"A biblically driven, beautiful a human. Dodson's honesty and vulnerability demonstrate that the key to leading through divisive times is to learn to suffer, grieve, and look to Christ. Every pastor who reads this book will learn principles and lessons to lead through divisive times, but even more, they will be moved by the kind of man and pastor Christ calls us to be in these difficult days. I heartily commend this book."

BRIAN CROFT, Executive Director, Practical Shepherding; Senior Fellow, Church Revitalization Center, Southern Baptist Theological Seminary

"This is an excellent book, offering much wisdom and insight to pastors who are facing unprecedented challenges. It is a masterful example of double listening: listening to the pastoral challenges of our time and listening to what the Spirit says to pastors in 2 Timothy. It arrives at just the right time, as I have increasingly engaged with leaders facing the same struggles that Jonathan Dodson skilfully addresses."

MICHAEL W. GOHEEN, PHD, Director of Theological Education, Missional Training Center, Pheonix

"If there ever was a time when the calling of a pastor could be called difficult, so much so that many are leaving the ministry at unprecedented rates, now is that time. In a world wracked with negativity, outrage, caricature, and us-against-them partisan tactics, Christ's undershepherds need a resource to help them navigate these realities with grace, truth, and integrity. This is that book!"

SCOTT SAULS, Senior Pastor, Christ Presbyterian Church, Nashville; Author, *Beautiful People Don't Just Happen*

"If you are wavering, if you are overwhelmed, if you have nothing left, read this book! *The Unwavering Pastor* will lift your head to see that we have an unwavering Father who is committed to you."

STEVE ROBINSON, Senior Pastor, Cornerstone Church, Liverpool, UK; Director, The Cornerstone Collective

"As a weary pastor myself, who is constantly talking to others in a similar condition, I appreciate how this book comes at the right time. Whatever trial you are leading others through at the moment, this book is sure to provide helpful instruction and life-giving encouragement."

TONY MERIDA, Pastor for Preaching and Vision, Imago Dei Church, Raleigh, North Carolina; Author, *Love Your Church*

"I sat down to read *The Unwavering Pastor* at the close of a particularly hard week in ministry. Jonathan's stories and gospel-rich reminders were a salve to my soul. I appreciate the stories and relatability as much as I value the grace and truth on every page. Any pastor or ministry leader who feels weighed down will find fresh encouragement here."

JEN OSHMAN, Author, *Cultural Counterfeits*

"Every pastor and Christian leader will relate to the poignant struggles so openly shared in this powerful book. Dodson has given all Christian leaders balm for our wounds and a compass through this storm."

TIMOTHY C. TENNENT, PHD, President and Professor of World Christianity, Asbury Theological Seminary

"Here is an oasis for pressured pastors and weary leaders. This book reads like a conversation with a good friend, who wants to prepare you for inevitable pain as well as save you from unnecessary pain. Jonathan writes from experience, sharing practical wisdom grounded in biblical insight. A timely book for our difficult times!"

ADAM RAMSEY, Lead Pastor, Liberti Church, Gold Coast, Australia; Network Director, Acts 29 Asia Pacific; Author, *Truth on Fire*

"A must-read for any and all who love, serve, and lead the local church. God has led the church through pandemics and divisions before, working through broken men and women just like us. *The Unwavering Pastor* is a reminder of God's faithfulness, guiding us toward hope."

JAY Y. KIM, Lead Pastor, WestGate Church, Silicon Valley; Author, *Analog Church*

"Gut-level honest, biblically rooted, beautifully written, and full of wise counsel. Pastor, read it to have your worries and wounds sympathetically understood, your weary soul encouraged, your calling clarified, and your love for Christ deepened. Again and again, I found fresh insights in these pages. For years, Jonathan Dodson has proven himself an important voice in matters of church and culture, and in this book, he shows himself to be a trustworthy pastor to pastors."

STEPHEN WITMER, Pastor, Pepperell Christian Fellowship, Massachusetts; Author, *A Big Gospel in Small Places*

"This book is timely because we are living in one of the most culturally challenging contexts of pastoral ministry in generations. This book is timeless because it flows from the inspired counsel Paul gives to Timothy as recorded in Scripture. Jonathan Dodson gives us help and hope by reminding us, as the apostle Paul did, the 'aim of our charge is love' (1 Timothy 1:5)."

DAVE BRUSKAS, US Director, Acts 29

"In my work as a counselor, I see pastors and ministry leaders facing anxiety, depression, weariness, panic attacks, and temptations to quit like never before. Jonathan honestly and vulnerably shares his own struggles, but he goes much further. He helps leaders endure controversy, division, criticism, and a whole host of cultural challenges alongside presenting a hopeful, practical, and encouraging vision forward. Every pastor would benefit from reading this gospel-rich encouragement."

JASON KOVACS, Executive Director, The Gospel Care Collective

"*The Unwavering Pastor* does a fantastic job in providing insightful counsel for pastors to depend on both God and others in ministry. The guidance in this must-read book will enrich steadfast and godly leaders to fulfill God's mission."

TOMMY LEE, Founder and President, Resource Global

"This is going to be a tremendous help for leaders serving Jesus. I recognize my own story here. Jonathan captured the emotional exhaustion, paralyzing emptiness, and spiritual confusion I felt when I experienced pastoral burnout at 50. Thankfully, Jonathan also gives us gospel balm and grace ballast. This short book is long on wisdom, grace, and timely encouragement."

SCOTTY SMITH, Pastor Emeritus, Christ Community Church, Franklin, Tennessee; Teacher-in-Residence, West End Community Church, Nashville, Tennessee

"As exhausting, and often spiritually depressing, as normal ministry may be, the last few years press us to go to deeper wells. This book is a deeper well—a very refreshing one."

MICHAEL HORTON, J. Gresham Machen Professor of Systematic Theology and Apologetics, Westminster Seminary, California

"Lyrical, subversive, tender, raw, grace-filled and profoundly counter-cultural, *The Unwavering Pastor* is a beautifully different book which speaks and embodies the gospel for this moment in a way in which we desperately need. Read it and drink deeply from its grace and truth."

GARY MILLAR, Principal, Queensland Theological College, Australia; Author, *Read This First*

"Pastors are facing discouragement and burnout at unprecedented rates, and the factors contributing to these challenges are complex. That's why I'm grateful for Jonathan Dodson's *The Unwavering Pastor*. This book brings a biblical wisdom and a surprising candor to helping pastors navigate the journey through the thicket of conflict, division, criticism, and even depression, always holding out the healing comfort of grace for the weary pastor's soul. This is a really good book."

JARED C. WILSON, Assistant Professor, Pastoral Ministry, Midwestern Seminary; Author, *Gospel-Driven Ministry*

THE
UNWAVERING
PASTOR

THE UNWAVERING PASTOR

Leading the Church with
Grace in Divisive Times

JONATHAN K. DODSON

The Unwavering Pastor
© Jonathan K. Dodson 2022

Published by:
The Good Book Company

thegoodbook.com | thegoodbook.co.uk
thegoodbook.com.au | thegoodbook.co.nz | thegoodbook.co.in

Cover design by Drew McCall

ISBN: 9781784987657 | Printed in India

To my fellow elders and friends,
Peter, Matt, and John

CONTENTS

FOREWORD

By Dane Ortlund

I needed this book. If you're a fellow weary pastor, you do too. And I didn't know how much I needed it until I read it.

Jonathan Dodson has already proven himself to be a wise and steady guide for the church today through his books and his ministry at City Life Church in Austin.

We don't need to be told what bizarre and perplexing times we live in. We know that. We need to be given guidance for how to negotiate these times as pastors. That's what Jonathan Dodson's *The Unwavering Pastor* gives us.

What kind of guide do I need and urgently welcome?

First, someone who is communing with God and commends that communion to us. To quote Francis Schaeffer, someone who knows the all-determining significance of "reality with God" for soul health—an actual moment-by-moment fellowship with the triune God. Sometimes books for ministry leaders have much incisive counsel but miss the nuclear core of communion with God. I was reminded time and again as I read of the freeing truth that all the obstacles of ministry are navigable if I walk through them with God. Jonathan brings us back repeatedly to this non-negotiable of pastoral health.

Second, someone who is biblical. But by "biblical" I don't mean someone who feeds Scripture into a family of other equally competing influences—cultural insights, common sense, personal experience, historical lessons, Barna surveys. I mean someone for whom the Bible is the all-determining treasure chest of truth and wisdom in how to lead fruitfully in these days. Jonathan is this.

Third, someone who is honest. Throughout the book Jonathan reflects on his own ministry experience with a refreshing transparency to which I can immediately relate. That candor builds trust as we read and serves us well.

Fourth, someone who is tested. It is obvious in these pages that Jonathan has been tried and found true. "Through many dangers, toils, and snares" he has already come. And we can learn from his experiences.

Fifth and finally, someone who writes well. Jonathan does.

The greatest temptation confronting every pastor right now is not one of resigning, though I know that many are contemplating that route (and if they do, Jesus won't love them any less). The greatest temptation is more subtle. It is to continue collecting a paycheck from the church while shifting our hearts into neutral. It is to carry forward the ministry at the level of activity, while quitting ministry in terms of our hearts and longings. This is the fork in the road that the criticism and adversities that Jonathan writes so poignantly about, and which we in the pastorate are facing more persistently than ever, presents us with.

Jonathan understands this greatest of temptations. He helped me understand it more acutely. And *The Unwavering Pastor* helps all of us, through these tumultuous times, fend off that ministry hypocrisy—smiling outside, quitting inside—as it is written by a man who is communing with God, biblical, honest, tested, and articulate.

I've only been a pastor for a few years. So I needed this book more than most. And already in that short time I have been tempted to waver: to withdraw—if not vocationally, in resignation, at least emotionally, in cynicism. God has kept me thus far, and this book is one means that will help me to keep going, dancing my way cheerfully through the Normandy Beach of pastoral ministry. If you read it with an open heart, unhurriedly and reflectively, then you will, like me, conclude your reading of this book deepened, freshly energized, and fortified with sage counsel as we all keep going.

Thank you for blessing us with this seasonable word, Jonathan.

Pastor Dane Ortlund
January, 2022

INTRODUCTION

You may have picked up this book because you want wisdom for leading others through complex cultural issues. There is certainly some of that here. Perhaps you're hoping to find a sympathetic ear from a fellow struggling pastor. I can promise you that. Maybe you want to know how to stay grounded when the world seems to be spinning out of control. If I haven't shown that, then I have failed.

What you will not find here is an unwavering pastor. I waver plenty: from troughs of despair to crests of spiritual joy, habitual sinner to faith-filled saint, ready-to-throw-in-the-towel leader to tenderhearted shepherd, perplexed pastor to confident leader. Christ has held on to me when my emotions would have taken me elsewhere. He has kept me when my sins could have easily swept me away.

Then in what sense can we be unwavering pastors and ministry leaders? In the sense that Paul meant when he said, "I know whom I have believed, and I am convinced that he is able to guard until that day what has been entrusted to me" (2 Timothy 1:12). What was Paul's unwavering confidence in? His faith? His spirituality? God's existence? No, his confidence was not in what he believed but who he believed in. He *knew* the God he trusted.

The more we know a person's character, the more we can discern their trustworthiness. And knowing the utter trustworthiness of God led Paul to tremendous confidence in God's commitment to the good news. Christ died, Christ rose, and Christ will come again to make all things new: even—especially—sinners. Paul's unwavering belief was in a God who forgives wavering people. It was the object of his trust that gave him confidence—the God of the gospel.

Therefore, his knowing, believing, and conviction are expressed as perfect verbs, meaning Paul's past knowledge, belief, and confidence continued on into his present. Why? Because he had encountered a God he could not "un-encounter." He was redeemed by a gospel that could not "un-redeem." He knew a messiah who is forever for and with him. Grace had left its mark.

An unwavering pastor's confidence doesn't come from their command of theology, his experience in counseling, or his faithful spiritual disciplines. Our confidence is derived from God's unwavering commitment to his own gospel, so that we can preserve, protect, and promote his grace in Christ through the Spirit for sinners. The triune God is unswervingly committed to that, and therefore, we can count on his steady presence, unrelenting forgiveness, unstoppable grace, and unmatched redemptive power. If you believe this, then you too can be an unwavering pastor.

How then do we lead his church with grace? I have taken two threads and tried to weave them together throughout this book. The first is an eternal thread—the inspired wisdom of Paul in his second letter to pastor Timothy. The first and fourth chapters contain remarkable candor about the hardships of ministry. Here is mature Paul, broken but full of hope, weak yet strengthened by Christ himself. The second and third chapters are full of penetrating insight for leading a church through division. Here is the sage dispensing wisdom to a growing pastor. It is a personally rich, theologically robust, practical letter.

The second thread is comprises my imperfect yet authentic pastoral reflections on how to lead the church—with grace—through divided times. It is virtually impossible to make it through division without sinning, and Christ is gladly present to remedy that. What is scary is that we can endure divisive times but emerge hardened and closed off. But when we allow God's grace to flow through us in these times, we soften and become more open-hearted toward fellow sinners. We draw near to God, and consequently, we love his people better and deeper. Though not easy, such a process is entirely worth it.

This book is, in a sense, a long prayer. A flaming arrow shot into the darkness of trial, with the hope that every leader who reads it, and every pastor who engages with it, will feel seen and known, not merely by me but by their Father in heaven and the compassionate Savior at his right hand. I hope you sense divine attentiveness, and even if you don't, that you will believe in it—and in a God who is always for you and not against you, especially when things are bleak.

~~~ 1 ~~~
DIVIDED TIMES

Covid is rampant. Hospitals are at capacity. The case count has skyrocketed and Stage 5 restrictions are clamping down—no leaving the house except for the essentials. Minneapolis is on fire, and injustice is in the streets.

I sit down at my writer's desk, wedged between the corner of our bedroom and a freshly made bed, and stare at the wall. Do I have to log on to another Zoom meeting? I'm reeling from meetings with people who think I'm not doing enough and those who think I'm doing too much. The topics of my failure seem to update as frequently as a Twitter timeline.

Overwhelmed, I open my laptop, and a notification pops up—another burning critique. It's a matter of time before this person leaves too. I try to remind myself that most people are grateful for our church, but the critics' voices grow louder and louder.

Division compounds the weight of ordinary leadership. It threatens the integrity of the thing you've given your life to. It's not a screw that needs to be tightened or a tire waiting to be aired up. It's a raging fire that, if not put out, burns the whole house down.

While there are always loose screws and slow leaks in life, people who divide are often so outwardly focused that they lose sight of their own issues. They ignore the telephone pole protruding from their own eye while obsessing over the speck in another's eye. When the telephone-polers take sides and attack, their logs collide violently with leaders. Caught between people on the left and the right, leaders suffer at the center of organizational ferment.

How do we lead through divisive times?

REFRESHING PEOPLE

The apostle Paul was no stranger to division. His second letter to Timothy mentions divisive people on every page. In an underground chamber, with a single hole overhead for light and air, he sits convicted of treason against Rome, awaiting execution. Apparently, instead of testifying in court to support Paul, Demas abandoned him for the love of this world. Many in Asia turned away from him, including Phygelus and Hermogenes. The sting of Alexander's betrayal is still fresh (2 Timothy 1:15, 4:10, 14). Where does Paul look for help in divided times? The answer may surprise you.

Paul reaches out: "To Timothy, my beloved child ... I long to see you, that I may be filled with joy" (1:2, 4). In crushing isolation, betrayed and forgotten by his spiritual co-workers, Paul looks *to the church* for help. While his letter is written to encourage and guide Timothy, it also provides a candid, intimate glimpse into Paul, who yearns to see the outline of Timothy's face and take in his joyful presence.

I preached yet another sermon to a cold, dark camera that week. Not a face in sight. On Sunday, our family logged off the pre-recorded service to prepare for lunch. Although we'd heard the word and sung to the Lord, discouragement lingered. I heard a honk, walked out onto the balcony, and leaned over. A grey minivan was parked below. A smiling face emerged. Peter, my friend and fellow elder, said, "Hey, we thought we would come see you and encourage you." Family members spilled out of the van. Emotion surged as tears filled my eyes. I called my family out to the balcony to talk with our friends below.

If social distancing has taught us anything, it's that we are made for one another. In his isolation, Paul longed to see Timothy. Paul mentions people *by name* 36 times in his brief second letter to Timothy: the same number of names mentioned in Romans, an epistle five times the length. Paul's old age and suffering worked like prescription lenses to clarify how important people are: Timothy, Lois, Eunice, Pudens, Linus, Claudia, and on. Men and women, leaders and members. Names, faces, stories, lives. People. Some brought him anguish; others brought him joy, but *all of them* mattered.

The apostle Paul "yearned" or "longed" for people. In addition to using this word to express his desire to see Timothy, he also longed for the Roman church (2 Timothy 1:11), the Thessalonians (1 Thessalonians 3:6), and the Philippians: "With God as my witness, I yearn for you with the affection of Christ Jesus" (1:8). Paul was free with his affection, but *longing* is something deeper. The Greek word *epipotheo* conveys not just a strong desire but "desire with the implication of need."[1] Paul didn't just plant each church; he needed the church. He wasn't merely supported by each church; he was *affectionately dependent* upon the church. He got close enough to people to receive joy from them: "Onesiphorus ... often refreshed me" (2 Timothy 1:16). It's interesting how people fill up their names with meaning. The root word of Onesiphorus means "to receive benefit from." He filled up his name, and the lives of others, with grace.

One way to thrive in ministry is to have an Onesiphorus or two. Peter is one of those people for me. We're quite different. He's a talented filmmaker, and I'm a pastor, but we both love movies. Good friends share good things in common, but great friends hold the greatest things in common. When two people delight in the same truth, it has a way of gluing them together. We frequently reflect on God's word together, marveling at who he is and what he is doing in our lives. But Peter also refreshes me by allowing me to be myself.

I'm not Pastor Jonathan. He knows that's a role I play: an important one but not the only one. He relates to me as a whole person, asking about my interests and family. I can speak freely with him about my struggles and know they will be held in confidence. And when we go to Alamo Drafthouse to see a movie, I don't have to be "on." If you don't have a Peter, ask God for one. They often refresh you.

My church is also a source of refreshment. During gathered worship some Sunday mornings, I am flooded with a sense of God's weighty presence and thrilling affection. This movement of the Spirit flows through the instruments, voices, liturgy, and prayers of our people, lifting my spirits and increasing my joy. On these occasions I find myself saying to the Lord, "This is why I do this, Lord. Thank you. Give me more of you."

But some weeks I don't feel like gathering with the church at all. Excuses spring to mind like tennis balls launched from a ball machine, but often it's in those very same weeks that I am most encouraged by the saints. In a particularly discouraging week, I considered canceling our City Group gathering but couldn't come up with a valid reason! When everyone arrived, they fell into effortless conversation. During our time of reflection, a couple who had endured significant loss declared, "We are so excited. God is at work. We can see it all around us!" I was so focused on my discouragement that I had lost sight of what God was doing. Sometimes we need a refreshing community to open our eyes to God's work.

Paul also found the church refreshing. He wrote to the Romans, "I appeal to you, brothers, by our Lord Jesus Christ and by the love of the Spirit, to strive together with me in your prayers to God on my behalf ... so that by God's will I may come to you with joy and be refreshed in your company" (Romans 15:30, 32). Appealing to their bond—loving Spirit and faithful Son—Paul sought refreshment from the church. Have you lost sight of this eternal bond, reducing the church to a vocational responsibility? Have you withheld your affection or need? Ask the church for prayer. Invite them to strive with you. Seek rejuvenating fellowship not only with your friends but also with your brothers and sisters in Christ.

WHEN PEOPLE LEAVE

In seeking refreshment from the church, we need not be naïve or idealistic. The same community that helps us can also hurt us. Paul's intimacy with the church also led to personal pain. He describes a painful visit to the Corinthians—so painful that he decided not to visit them again. Instead, he wrote them a letter "so that when I came I might not suffer pain from those who should have made me rejoice" (2 Corinthians 2:3). In a raw display, Paul shows us the cost of affectionate dependence—those who should bring us joy can also inflict pain. He writes, "For I wrote to you out of much affliction and anguish of heart and with many tears" (v 4). Just one phrase would have communicated his pain clearly, but he includes three to express just how much the church hurt him: much affliction, anguish of heart, many tears. Leading the church means living close enough to others to get hurt.

I opened my email and saw a note from a friend in the church and eagerly clicked on it. I was skewered by what I read. He and his family were leaving the church. Leaving churches is part of life in America. There are good and bad reasons to leave a church, but departures are inevitable, especially in a geographically mobile society. Early in my pastorate I resented this, but eventually God helped me accept the transience involved in pastoring an urban community. He even reframed it for me, helping me to see the turnover in terms of providence—God fixes the times and places where people live so that others can hear the gospel (Acts 17:26-27). I began to see goings as sendings. We pastor people as long as we have them and then send them off to take the gospel to the next place.

However, not all goings are sendings. Some are just *leavings*, and leavings like this one hurt. Leaving like what? Leaving like you're not friends when you are friends. At least that's what I thought. This person had pursued me and asked me to spend more time with him. I walked him through some sin struggles and watched him mature into a godly man who led others. My wife and I really clicked with him and his wife—a rare thing in a changing community, so we cultivated a friendship with them. We went to concerts, went out for dinner, hung out as guys and gals, and ministered to the church by their side. Then I got an email—an email—announcing their departure. Don't friends talk about this stuff? I scheduled a painful visit.

I met Tom and another elder at Merit Coffee Co., a clean, white, urban coffee shop with sprawling seating and great espresso.[2] After the awkward greetings, we sat down to talk through the reasons why they had chosen to leave. I empathized where I could and challenged him where I felt I should. It was a heartfelt discussion, but I walked away wincing. You see, this awkward leaving was one in a whole string of friends leaving the church. Some went through bitter attack and insult; others just disappeared. There was no conversation—not even an email. Just poof and they were gone. My heart was done.

For the first time in ministry, I was genuinely tempted to close up my heart. I told myself I would love the church, counsel the church, pray for the church, and preach the gospel to the church as best as I could, but I would no longer *befriend the church*. Friends would be found elsewhere. Until I read Psalm 62:1: "For God alone my soul waits in silence; from him comes my salvation. He alone is my rock and my salvation, my fortress; I shall not be greatly shaken."

I couldn't get past the first three words: for God *alone*. I knew "alone" all right, but not really with God. I had waited in silence; actually I cried out in silence but not with God as my salvation. Sometimes we want God plus. God plus a spouse. God plus a friend. God plus a job. I wanted God minus. God minus the pain. God minus the suffering. God minus the abandonment. God minus friends treating me like a spiritual commodity: sought after when I'm needed—disposed of when a better prospect comes along. But the Spirit was saying, *God alone*.

In God, alone, is our salvation. He is our rock and our fortress, not friendship. God was saying, *Friendship is not a fortress. People are not your protection. I am your safety; I am your refuge, and I will never leave.* Then I read, "Trust in him at all times, O people; pour out your heart before him" (v 8). Don't board up your heart; pour it out to him. I knew I could trust the Lord, so I let it rip. I shared the pain, and he comforted me; I confessed my sin, and he not only forgave me but also loved me in my mess. You can trust *him* at all times. There is no better prospect. *Friendship isn't a fortress; God is a fortress*—a marvelous one at that. God's presence is so dependable that it enables us to give ourselves in serving those who disappoint us.

Paul's painful experience with the Corinthians wasn't a one-off. He describes his prosecution in Rome: "At my first defense no one came to stand by me, but all deserted me" (2 Timothy 4:16). Desertion is an intense word. Jesus used this word in the sixth hour of his crucifixion to describe his feeling *forsaken* by God (Mark 15:34). It is important for leaders to verbalize these feelings to a friend, spouse, or counselor, and especially to God. Paul didn't keep his sense of abandonment a secret. His letter is littered with names of people who went poof: Demas, Phygelus and Hermogenes, Hymenaeus and Philetus (2 Timothy 1:15, 20; 2:17; 4:10), and Alexander the coppersmith, who "did me great harm" (4:14). This is the last letter Paul wrote, and he was still writing lines like that. Betrayal stings, even years later.

But Paul didn't close off his heart to the church, no matter how much it hurt. He declares, "May it not be charged against them!" (4:16). That is not my first response when I am betrayed. I reach for the imprecatory justice-seeking psalms. I wonder if Paul did too, when the gavel came down and his sentence was announced. Yet he refused to hold the church's betrayal against them. He didn't stew in bitterness but soaked in grace. He sounds like our Lord, who from a blood-stained cross said, "Father, forgive them, for they know not what they do" (Luke 23:24).

How did Paul not hold their betrayal against them? It seems superhuman... because it is. Paul forgave his betrayers and willed no ill against them because there was one person who did not abandon *him*: "But the Lord stood by me and strengthened me" (2 Timothy 4:17). The word "stood" is chosen carefully. No one stood up for Paul when he was on trial. But when everyone else left, the Lord Jesus remained. When false witnesses hurled accusations, Jesus stood by him as a witness of his faithfulness. Jesus also stands by you. He is not embarrassed to do so. Rather, he proudly stands next to his faithful servants. Jesus remains when people leave.

When loving the church left Paul with wounds, Jesus stuck around to bandage him up. Jesus doesn't minister in word only. He serves Paul. He bends down to lift Paul up and imparts strength to his weary servant. This ministry is not only for Paul but also for us. Jesus bends down to minister to us. When we are low, he goes lower to lift us up. Jesus sympathizes with your struggle. Will you receive his strength and believe in his heart for you? Collapse into his arms if you have to and receive the ministry of Jesus!

Paul led through thick and thin because he knew the Lord was with his spirit (2 Timothy 4:22). Instead of boarding up his soul, he continued to long for the church with the affection of Christ Jesus. His longing wasn't self-manufactured; it sprang from the love of the Holy Spirit, who imparted Jesus' affection for him. Through this intimacy with Jesus—"For God, alone, my soul waits"—Paul not only received but recycled God's perfect love. He saw his betrayers' departure as an invitation into depths of intimacy with the Spirit and the Son. If we accept this invitation, *Jesus Christ* will love the church through us.

PRAYING GRATEFULLY

How did Paul persevere in ministry to the very end? In the same way he begins and ends this pain-laced letter— with prayer. He does not begin by complaining about how he has been mistreated. He starts off with thanksgiving because he has developed a habit of thinking beyond himself. His prayers are filled with people and not with *Dear God, sort out so and so.* Instead, he begins by thanking God for *specific* people. He expresses gratitude for *Timothy's* sincere faith, and in savoring his faith, Paul tips over into gratitude for the faith of Timothy's *mother* and *grand-mother*—Eunice and Lois (1:3-5). Who can you thank God for right now? Which people have been a grace to you in this season of ministry?

"Faith" is shorthand for the gospel.[3] Paul praises God because the gospel has moved into the lives of these saints. It didn't stay on the outside—a mere doctrine to affirm or liturgy to rehearse. The gospel took up residence in them. This kind of faith is unlike the cold, combative Christianity often caricatured on our screens. It is regenerative, warm, and lively. Christ moved *noticeably* into the lives of Lois, Eunice, and Timothy. No wonder Paul's thanking God!

Have you ever looked at a photograph and marveled at what the photographer captured? Good photographers aren't in a hurry. They are observant. With eyes wide open, they take in their surroundings to capture what happens in the moment. To remember people in prayer, we must slow down to take in what God is doing in them. To pray gratefully for the church, we must see people, not just serve them.

Prayer is an opportunity for close-ups. Gratitude zooms in on what God is doing and praises him for it. When I'm praying with a small group of people, I am often moved when I hear someone praise God for a specific quality in another person's life. They pick up on the character of God in others and credit him for it. I see others through their lens, and it stirs the soul. Eugene Peterson says, "Giving thanks is one of the most attractive things that we can do." But it's not *just* attractive; it attracts us to God. Praying gratefully for others leads us to appreciate them and the God they serve. As Peterson says, "Praise is our best work."[4]

Praising God is easy when you're praying for the righteous, but what about praying for the critical? Paul advises pastors to patiently endure evil and correct opponents with gentleness (2:24-25). I don't know how to do this apart from through prayer. When I'm not praying for my critics, it's much easier to find fault and demonize than be patient and gentle.

During an unusually tense time in our church, a small group of progressively minded people began critiquing my sermons. They often took words out of context, distorted my intended meaning, and took offense. I scheduled meetings to better understand where they were coming from. I fielded angry, irrational emails, but the criticism only kept coming. As a consequence, I developed a significant awareness of how my sermon vocabulary choices could affect this group. It was demoralizing to go into the pulpit knowing people were poised to misunderstand and misconstrue my words, instead of seeking to understand and cherish the word of God.

During that time, while I was brushing my teeth in the morning, the faces of my critics would pop into my mind, their jabs and critiques on replay in my thoughts. Each time I thought of a person, I had a choice: follow the criticism down the rabbit hole and mount a defense, or pray for each person. I quickly learned that rehearsing counter arguments didn't endear me to them, so each time a face popped up I began to pray for them. I prayed they would repent; I prayed they would not cause division, but I also prayed they would know the heart-melting love of Jesus.

I also learned it wasn't enough to pray for them once; I had to pray for them every time their faces popped up or I would grow defensive and bitter. But prayer for my critics made me gentler and more patient. It softened my heart toward them, and I know God heard every prayer. Of course, it wasn't my praying that changed me. It was Jesus, who stood by me, who sustained me, who taught me not to charge it to their account. It's hard to hate those whom we carry to the Lord of love in prayer.

PRAYING CONSTANTLY

Paul also teaches us to pray constantly: "I remember you constantly in my prayers night and day" (1:3). He prayed all the time at any time. Now we might object: what else did Paul have to do in prison? But doesn't that make his constant prayer for others, not himself, more noteworthy? When I feel isolated and hurt, my thoughts don't naturally go toward others. They tend to be about me. But here is Paul, in a hole in the ground, *interceding for others*. One commentator notes, "His whole waking being was in a spirit of intercession."[5] I love that. I want to live like that—attuned to the Spirit in dependent prayer with every breath.

Praying constantly can be hard, especially in hectic seasons of division. One reason why we find it difficult was anticipated in *Wired* magazine nearly 20 years ago, when Michael Goldhaber, "the internet prophet you've never heard of," predicted that the internet would drown us in information, making attention so diffuse that an "attention economy" would be formed.[6] He further predicted that when this economy matured, its "increasing demand for our limited attention would keep us from reflecting, or thinking deeply."[7]

Prayer requires reflection; we often live by reaction. After you wake up, what is one of the first things you do? Reflect or absorb the news? When you stop at a light, do you reflect on the day or check your cradle-secured phone? While you're driving, do you listen to a podcast or playlist, or pray for others? When you're waiting in line, do you check Instagram, Twitter, or Facebook? When you go to bed, do you reflect, pray, or doomscroll? No wonder we find it hard to pray without ceasing. We're too busy getting our attention stolen.

What could it look like to take our attention back? To be a waking, praying being? I find it helpful to turn off digital inputs to create space for spiritual input. Create space for memories and then *turn memories into prayers*. When Paul remembers Timothy, he turns his memory into a prayer. When you remember someone in the in-between spaces, pray for them. When you're longing for community, pray for people in your community. When you think, "I sure miss so and so", pause and pray for them. Don't dead-end in nostalgia or fantasy. *Follow your memories into prayers.*

When I am prompted to pray for someone throughout the day, I occasionally send that person a text. Very often, they respond by saying it was just what they needed to hear. Cultivate the habit of turning memories into prayers and you'll find yourself praying constantly.

PASTORING IN POWER

A survey by the Barna Group reveals that, in 2021, 38 percent of Protestant pastors gave "real, serious consideration to quitting being in full-time ministry."[8] Many resigned. All leaders struggled. Where do we get the power to lead through divided times?

Ministry of Affirmation

To help Timothy lead through division, Paul affirms Timothy by expressing confidence in him: "I am reminded of your sincere faith, a faith that dwelt first in your grandmother Lois and your mother Eunice and now, *I am sure, dwells in you* as well" (1:5, my italics). This isn't a throwaway line. He praises the lively, indwelling faith of Timothy's esteemed mother and grandmother and then adds Timothy to the group!

Over the years mentors I respect have said five simple, powerful words to me: "I am proud of you." These words are meaningful not because they mean I'm awesome but because they convey approval from someone I respect. Affirmation is especially powerful when it comes from people we admire. Towering in our estimation, mentors pull us up with their words.

Their endorsement is even more significant when it's tied to the work of God in our lives. After all, what we want most is not to be people's favorite leader but to honor and please the King of kings and the Lord of lords. Paul nails this "gospel" affirmation when he says, "I am sure [that the faith] dwells in you." In using the perfect tense of "convince" ("I am sure"), he is saying, *I was convinced, I am convinced, and I continue to be convinced that the gospel is alive in you!* It's so powerful to hear words like this when we are drowning in criticism. So, if you see someone honoring and pleasing the Lord, tell them you are proud of them. Highlight God's work in their ministry. If you don't have a mentor in your life, look for one and tell them you are looking for affirmation, as well as constructive feedback. If your team doesn't practice godly affirmation, you may need to start by setting an example of godly encouragement to them.

Can I give you a dose of affirmation? The crazy thing about Paul's affirmation is that Timothy wasn't killing it in leadership. He lacked some typical leadership qualities. He wasn't bold and courageous but fearful and timid. Yet, even though Timothy had some things to work on, Paul knew his struggle wasn't a reflection of his true self. He knew the true, life-from-death Tim was indwelt with the gospel, which tells us that *God*—the Creator of quarks and strings and atoms, and gravity and black holes and galaxies, and stunning sunsets—so loves you that he chose to die in your place *and* triumph over your greatest enemy. God is *your* defender, down to the death.

The gospel affirms us even more deeply. The good news is that you are God's dwelling place. Yep, you are where God chooses to kick back. Not just you, all the saints, but also you personally. The Holy—*holy*—Spirit chooses to reside in you (Ephesians 2:22). He occupies the most intimate place in our lives and does it without regret. Take a deep breath and inhale his heavenly affirmation.

Ministry of Exhortation
When we're struggling, sometimes we need exhortation more than we need affirmation. With critics breathing

down his neck, Timothy could have easily dwelt on what they thought of him, even living in fear of their opinions. But Paul exhorts Timothy "to fan into flame the gift of God, which is in you through the laying on of my hands, for God gave us a spirit not of fear but of power and love and self-control" (2 Timothy 1:6-7). He reminds Timothy of a gift so powerful that it displaces fear and compels love.

What gift could he be talking about? Paul could be referring to a spiritual gift or Timothy's ordination. However, he says the gift is "in you" not "with you," and it's a gift that came into Timothy through the laying on of hands. The gift people received when Paul laid hands on them in Acts was the Holy Spirit. So when Paul says, "fan into the flame the gift," he is exhorting Timothy to be his true self—the Tim indwelt by the Spirit, who has "not a [S]pirit of fear but of power, love, and self-control."[9]

The old Timothy is tempted by fear, timidity, and self-doubt, but the Spirit-Timothy is filled with power, love, and self-control to suffer for the gospel. Paul is essentially saying, *Your critics don't define who you are. Your feelings of fear and apprehension don't have the last word. What defines you is who lives in you! You're a life-from-death, Spirit-indwelt child of God.* We have exactly what we need to lead through difficult times; we just need to fan the flame.

How do we fan the flame? The word for "fan into flame" combines two Greek words: one for "life" and the other for "fire". The fire of the Spirit isn't a destructive flame but a life-giving force that brings warmth and light into our souls. It means "to kindle afresh." Have the embers of your soul grown dim? Take some time to stoke the fire of the Spirit.

When I kindle the fire in my fireplace, I look for space beneath the logs to blow on the embers. Perhaps you need to create space in your day to blow on the Spirit. This might entail going for a walk and talking to the Spirit about your challenges and heartaches. Alternatively, you may need to throw another log on the fire. This may mean placing Scripture on your heart and praying for it to ignite. But don't throw too much Scripture on or you will snuff out the fire. Let your soul breathe. Thomas Watson warns, "Too often we walk away from the Word of God coldhearted because we fail to warm our souls at the fires of meditation."[10] When we fan into flame the gift of the Spirit, we make a deliberate effort to receive from the Spirit who we are in Christ.

An unwavering pastor remains centered in adversity by developing friendships that bring refreshment, while also remembering that friendship is not a fortress. God is our refuge. Unwavering pastors pray constantly and gratefully, heeding valid critiques but zooming in on signs of God's goodness. They stay afloat in a deluge by clinging to gospel affirmation and heeding exhortation, giving God's words more weight than their critics' words, choosing to live by the power and presence of the Spirit.

THE UNWAVERING PASTOR

An unwavering pastor navigates divided times by:

- developing refreshing friendships.

- remembering that friendship isn't a fortress but that God is our refuge.

- using prayer to zoom in on God's goodness and express gratitude.

- turning memories into prayers and mental images into intercession.

- giving and receiving gospel affirmation and exhortation.

- fanning the flame of the indwelling Spirit.

～～～ *2* ～～～

QUESTIONING CHRISTIANITY

In seminary I was trained to answer questions like: Is the Bible reliable? Did Jesus really rise from the dead? Are miracles really possible? Each question is driven by the same important underlying question: is Christianity *true*? However, today people often ask different questions. Considering the prospect of celibacy, my friend with same-sex attraction asks, "Does God want me to be lonely and unloved?" A frustrated person of color proclaims, "Preaching the gospel isn't enough. We need justice!" A woman in my city group inquires, "Why does it seem like the church is against women?" They are essentially asking: Is the Bible sexist? Is Christianity racist? Is the church homophobic?

These three issues—sexuality, race, and gender—are *the* issues of our time.[11] Each one was supercharged by a lightning-rod event, all of which occurred within the span of five years, placing tremendous weight on ministry leaders.[12] Yet beneath these questions is an even deeper question: is Christianity *good*? People want to know if the new life Christianity offers is actually a good life.[13]

How should we respond?

PASTORAL APOLOGETICS

We can respond to controversial topics by making book recommendations, but the issues are deeply personal. We could respond with packed one-liners, but the issues are also complex. We could update our statement of faith, but application is messier than tidy doctrinal statements. When questions are raised about our church's views on women in ministry, racial bias, and sexual orientation, I try to remind myself that behind the often-barbed inquiries is that deeper question: is Christianity good?

While we should respond to cultural concerns with biblically grounded theological answers, our response should also offer tangible proof of Christianity's goodness.[14] We must also respond *pastorally*, paying close attention not only to what we say but *how* we say it. The way we respond can be a defense of the goodness of Christian faith. When thorny issues arise will you be combative or kind? When church members complain will you be dismissive or attentive? Will you truly listen and embody the goodness of Christ in your response? People need more than apologetic zingers, book recommendations, and tidy statements of faith. They need flesh-and-blood leaders with the character of Christ, who carefully consider the issues. They need *pastoral* apologetics.

Pastoral apologetics pairs a reasonable, biblical response to an issue with a charitable and winsome spirit. It embodies both the truth *and* goodness of the gospel. While enduring his share of church division, Timothy received these striking words: "The Lord's servant must not be quarrelsome but kind to everyone, able to teach, patiently enduring evil, correcting his opponents with gentleness"

(2 Timothy 2:24-25). If we are bound to Jesus, not public opinion, we will teach his word in this way: with kindness, patience, and gentleness. *This* is pastoral apologetics. As servants of the Lord, we should defend both the news *and* goodness of the gospel.

What does pastoral apologetics look like in practice? It is virtue with action: kindness while arguing, patience amid evil, gentleness when correcting. Often we choose either action or virtue: correction, instruction, and argument *or* kindness, patience, and gentleness. Depending on our proclivity, we tend to either defend the faith or pastor the people. But Paul calls us to both: to pastoral apologetics. To be kind, not just to those we like but to those who are quarrelsome. To be able to teach, not only when we are praised but also when we are opposed. To correct the teachable and deal gently with the proud. This is the real—essential—challenge: to hold action and virtue together when the heat is on. *This* is leadership for tense times.

Kind, Not Quarrelsome

"Kind not quarrelsome" reminds me of an elder who met with an angry married couple in our church. As the couple voiced their concerns, they misjudged the elder and mischaracterized the church. It appeared they were trying to sabotage their relationship with the church. Instead of defending himself, this elder calmly zeroed in on the real issue. He implored the couple to move forward with him in "love that endures all things." His robust kindness was a Neo-like hand before a hail of bullets. Personal attacks seemed to fall to the ground.[15]

Paul's instruction assumes the presence of a quarrel but insists on the absence of a quarreling spirit. In conflict we must talk, or even argue, but we must do so kindly. However, we often choose between being quarrelsome or nice. We may defend the truth while sacrificing peace or make peace while sacrificing the truth. But in choosing one over the other, we lose the spirit of Jesus. We settle for aggression or niceness.

President of Biola College, Dr. Barry Corey, clarifies the difference between aggression and niceness: "Whereas aggression has a firm center and hard edges, niceness has soft edges and a spongy center. Niceness may be pleasant, but it lacks conviction. It has no soul. Niceness trims its sails to prevailing cultural winds and wanders aimlessly, standing for nothing and thereby falling for everything."[16] The Lord's servant possesses a firm center with soft edges, a kind, not quarrelsome spirit.

How did the elder exude such kindness? He was kind because, in the moment, Christ mattered more to him than self-respect. His aim wasn't to win but to love. He was truthful because he wasn't a slave to the couple's opinion. He exuded mind-boggling kindness because he acted *as a servant of the Lord*. He knew that by serving the Lord, in word and deed, he would best serve his hostile brother and sister. Enslaved to Christ, he sought that "God may perhaps grant them repentance" (2 Timothy 2:25). His Christ-like response was a compelling defense of the goodness of Christianity.

Patient with Evil

In any church gathering, evil lurks about. Some Sundays, sitting in my chair bent over in prayer, I can sense fiery arrows descending upon the congregation. Occasionally, I feel the presence of a huge, invisible finger pointing at my head. Words of condemnation spring to mind: *So and so isn't going to believe a word you say. This sermon isn't any good.* Some days, thank God, I sense no evil at all. But the tempter is always on the move.

A good leader is aware of the traps laid for those he leads. He doesn't just preach the text or against the headlines but instructs *his* congregation. He is attentive to the evil that besets his flock. It might be distorted ideas about race, sex, or gender, or it may be anxiety, condemnation, or the occult. Whatever the issue, our attentiveness shouldn't stop with calling out sinister influences.

A *patient* leader separates the evil traps from struggling saints. He knows that those who fall into evil are more than the sum total of their sins. He chooses to see them as disciples in need of instruction—wandering sheep who require a shepherd. As a result, he preaches against sin, but for the sinner. He pries open the trap while pointing them to freedom. This puts considerable strain on the leader—patience in the face of evil does not come easily— but it is worth it for the freedom of even a single soul.

Bobby is a hefty six-foot-two struggler. The first day he visited our church, he plopped down on the first row wearing a green-and-white hockey jersey. His stringy white hair and dark countenance stood out. I was imme- diately compelled to pray silently for him. Later, I discov- ered he was financially destitute and living out of his car. Within months of heeding gospel preaching and immers- ing himself in our Christian community, his countenance lifted. He got a job and an apartment, but most of all, Christ got him.

A couple of years later, I noticed some people in our church drifting into old sins, so I decided to preach on the dangers of returning to the old self. I urged the church to be their true selves—to live as God's new creation. Afterwards, I caught up with Bobby outside. He looked confused and down. He shared that he had fallen back into the occult, consulting tarot cards and palm-readers, searching for a spiritual hit. I had no idea he had an occult-tangled past, but the Holy Spirit did. He alerted me to the evil traps of past sins, so strugglers could wriggle free. Bobby escaped evil that week.

Sometimes patience with evil means praying against a felt presence. At other times it's simply heeding the Holy Spirit, unaware of what evil lurks. It can also mean putting up with the impact of the latest headline without getting embroiled in it, or absorbing unfounded criticism from partisan church members, refusing to get dragged into political debate, or enduring the scorn of conspiracy theorists, while refusing to go down the YouTube rabbit hole. Paul wisely states, "Have nothing to do with foolish, ignorant controversies; you know that they breed quarrels" (2 Timothy 2:23).

The patient-with-evil leader refuses to make the church his enemy. While attentive to temptation trends in the church, he doesn't aim sermons at individuals. He renounces the bully pulpit, refusing to use his words to vindicate himself. Instead, he preaches God's word with God's grace. He chooses to pastor like a doctor dealing with sickness, attacking the disease, not the patient. His abiding concern is to make the patient well—to teach and pray so people can become whole.

Correcting with Gentleness

If we are truly patient with evil, we will also respond gently to our critics. Several years ago, I made a general observation that passion for social justice in the American church seemed to be eclipsing a pursuit of personal holiness. I tweeted, "There seems to be an abundance of boldness on matters of social justice but not on matters of personal holiness." My desire was to correct an imbalance by encouraging boldness in both areas: personal holiness and social justice. Personal holiness without active concern for justice fails to reflect the full extent of God's holiness. Social justice without a robust commitment to personal holiness leads to self-righteous, unjust behavior. It was not the most well-crafted tweet I've written, and as you might imagine, it garnered some pushback. One person in our church responded by tweeting that holiness and justice aren't mutually exclusive. I whimsically affirmed her observation. The tweets touched a nerve.

In my mind, her observation clearly didn't apply to us. She was well acquainted with the vision of our church—"to renew cities socially, spiritually, and culturally with the gospel of Jesus"—and our active mercy and justice ministries. However, tension and criticism continued to build after the online exchange until an elder and I met with her and her friend. In that meeting, she expressed frustration and hurt because of my response to her on Twitter. She explained to me that, as a Hispanic, she felt that I was saying her opinion didn't matter and that I was shutting down the conversation. That was not my intent, but the damage had been done. Now was the time for gentleness.

I apologized for making her feel belittled and reassured her that I valued her as a sister in Christ, a leader, and a member of a minority. I continued to ask her questions to better understand some of her concerns regarding racial injustice. It was a helpful and reconciliatory meeting. It was also sanctifying. While I was right to correct an imbalance, God also corrected my racial insensitivity through her. He nurtured gentleness in correction.

Which of these areas in pastoral apologetics do you need to mature in? Being kind but not quarrelsome? Patiently instructing in evil? Giving gentle correction to opponents? Is there an area where you need to pause and repent?

Receiving Criticism

When we receive criticism, it is important to weigh what is said and not dismiss it. Pastor Tim Shorey says we should receive a critique with *the assumption* that we are wrong![17] Wrong? How? In opinion, attitude, word choice, emphasis, tone, grasp of the information, or timing. Imagine how this posture would embody goodness. Think of its potential to diffuse explosive conflict. Consider its Christ-like humility.

Each time I receive criticism, I try to listen carefully to see if there is anything I can learn. Even if a lot of what is said is untrue, I try to look for a kernel of truth. But, honestly, sometimes it's really hard. It can be painful to sort through false accusations to find a splinter of truth. I don't always succeed, which is one reason why I take serious critiques to our elders. It's helpful to receive their counsel so I can avoid responding defensively. Trusted peers can validate or challenge us as necessary. Of course, being kind doesn't mean not standing up for the truth. It means speaking the truth with a humble heart.

Pastoral apologetics can make a tremendous difference in divided times. However, it may take years to see the fruit, and sometimes, we won't see the results at all. Then why should we do the hard work? Because we are *the Lord's servants*.

TAKE THE LONG VIEW

When I asked the most gracious pastor I know for advice in pastoral ministry, he said, "Take the long view of people." Too often we judge people on the madness of a single moment or a crazy season of life, when what they need is a pastor who will take a long, gracious view of who they are becoming. And not only who they are becoming but also who they will one day be. What if we treated people not only from their sin forward but also from their glory backward? What if we shepherded people as they are in Christ? Our leadership would soften, helping us pastor graciously through complex, contested issues.

Discipling One Gay Man

When people come out as gay, lesbian, or transgender, they often say something like "I was hiding my true self all these years. Now I'm owning my truth." Actor Ellen Page, who came out as Elliot Page, a trans man, is quoted as saying, "I can't begin to express how remarkable it feels to finally love who I am enough to pursue my authentic self."[18] I struggled to understand this pent-up inauthenticity, until I met George.

I met George in rehab. He was penniless, shoeless, lonely, strung-out, and gay.[19] After speaking with him for a while, I asked if I could bring him some shoes and a Bible. He welcomed the shoes and half-heartedly accepted the Bible. We spent many hours together discussing his broken dreams and deep, unfulfilled longings. Eventually, we talked about his same-sex attraction. As our relationship deepened, he shared how he felt about his sexuality: "The thought of being with a woman makes my skin crawl." That was a gut punch. Although I couldn't relate, I knew it was true for him. Hearing this helped me appreciate just how deep his struggle was. Then one afternoon, after discussing Genesis 1 – 2 with him, George asked, "Does God want me to be lonely and unloved the rest of my life?" That, too, was eye-opening. When we slow down to pastor people, not just beliefs, we inevitably learn how to pastor better.

I empathized with him as best as I could and then asked him what he was looking for in love. He described a relationship based on unconditional acceptance and intimate companionship—something no human could give him perfectly but what every single one of us longs for. I sympathetically pointed out that God invented love because he is love—a reality created, sustained, and satisfied perfectly by him. Certainly, God did not want George or anyone with same-sex attraction to be lonely. He feels so strongly about this that he sent his Son to die in our place, not only to forgive our sins but also to welcome *anyone* who trusts in him into his divine, undying love. I asked George, if he could trust this God with his soul, could he also trust him with his sexuality? He reluctantly agreed.

Eventually, George repented of his sin and placed his faith in Jesus. Afterwards, he asked if he could get baptized in his apartment pool so his city group could join in celebrating with him. Lowering him into the turquoise water, I baptized him in the name of the Father, Son, and Holy Spirit. He emerged from the pool with a shout of joy. George distanced himself from gay relationships and threw himself into the church community. He frequently baked for his city group, brought others to church, and met with me for discipleship. He became an active part of our church.

After a few years, George moved away and cut off contact with us, and a year later married another man. Then one morning, he walked into his living room to find his partner hanging from the ceiling, with an electrical cord wrapped around his neck. His partner's suicide sent George into a frenzy.

In need of familiarity and a supportive community, he moved back to Austin. We began meeting again. I counseled him through the pain of his loss. Slowly, George began to heal and reengage with his faith. He started coming to church services again, eventually bringing friends with him. I was kind and loving toward these men, but they were clearly more than friends. I knew it was extremely difficult for George to resist his same-sex attraction, so I encouraged him to fight his temptation to have sex with them. But after one boyfriend disappeared, another would quickly appear.

George was falling into a persistent pattern of sexual sin. I knew that if I truly loved him, I had to confront him. As

I was praying one afternoon, the Spirit compelled me to drop by George's house. After some chitchat I said to him, "George, you know your relationships are not pleasing to the Lord."

"Says who?" he retorted.

"Says Scripture," I responded.

"That's just how you interpret it," he replied.

Then I said to him, my heart thumping rapidly, "No, that's 1 Corinthians: the sexually immoral and men who practice homosexuality will not inherit the kingdom of God" (1 Corinthians 6:9). He stared at me angrily and started for the stairs.

"George, I love you enough to say this: God will judge you for this if you do not repent. Please turn to him."

We haven't spoken in years.

This is a painful story to tell because I love George. I spent so much time with him that he became a spiritual son to me. To this day, I have to hold back tears as I think about him. I know I was patient with evil. I sought to correct him with gentleness, with the hope that he would escape the snare of the devil and return to the Lord.

George witnessed an undeniable apologetic—the love of God through the body of Christ. He was so convinced of God's love in the church that he brought numerous friends to Sunday gatherings. This long-haul love inadvertently addressed Christians in our church who struggle to embrace the Bible's view on homosexuality. But embodying the love of Christ did not come without cost.

I was shamed by pastors for not being harder on him and scorned by non-Christians for saying anything at all. Through this I learned not to be ashamed of the testimony of our Lord, who died and rose so homosexual and heterosexual disciples can cherish his companionship more than their sexual desires. I pray that my consistent witness to the love of Christ and my gentle but firm correction echo in George's heart. May the Lord grant him repentance, leading him back to a knowledge of the truth.

THE TESTIMONY OF JESUS

A spiritual leader's calling is unpopular and our ministry often unwelcome. Sometimes we are rejected by the world, and at other times we are scorned by the church. Paul experienced both, leading him to say, "Therefore do not be ashamed of the testimony about our Lord, nor of me his prisoner, but share in suffering for the gospel by the power of God" (2 Timothy 1:8). His chains were the result of Roman persecutions and his pain because of abandonment by some Christians. How did he remain true to the testimony of Jesus?

A testimony is verbal evidence for some truth claim. The apostles gave their testimonies as evidence for the hope of resurrection life (Acts 4:33). Jesus witnessed to the inbreaking kingdom of God, which welcomes repentant sinners. Moses presided over a tent of witness (*martyrion*), as he spoke on God's behalf, in order for God to relate to Israel (LXX, Exodus 33:7-11). These "martyrs" were willing to stand up for the truth, despite the rejection they endured from their own people. Why? Their testimonies pointed to life through death, when heaven meets earth, and God speaks with man—testimonies fulfilled in Jesus: life comes out of death, heaven overlaps earth, and God welcomes man in Christ Jesus! Martyrs so cherished these eternal truths that they let the chips fall where they may.

How do we testify to the gospel when the cost seems so high? By recognizing that we suffer not as prisoners of the world but as slaves of Christ. Paul writes, "Do not be ashamed of the testimony about our Lord, *nor of me his prisoner*" (my italics). He considered his chains to be Christian, not Roman. So also is each of us the Lord's prisoner. Our sufferings are not the random results of political conflict or ethical disagreement but providential appointments for gospel advance. So, when you suffer, remember that even your chains do not belong to your opponents. In the hands of the Lord, they are bitter occasions for sweeter intimacy with Jesus. They are opportunities to pastor more like Jesus and with Jesus.

As servants of the Lord, we have been commissioned to show a questioning world the truth and goodness of Christianity. This requires taking the view of others that God himself takes of us—a long, patient, hopeful view. It also means standing up for the testimony of Jesus in the power of God. May our disillusioned world see in us a Christianity that is not only good but good *because it's true*.

THE UNWAVERING PASTOR

Unwavering pastors respond to those who question Christianity by:

- being kind, patient, and humble with those who disagree with us.

- assuming we are wrong in some way in conflict, not always right.

- taking a long view of those hurt by Christians and responding to them gently.

- embracing gospel martyrdom—being a sacrificial witness to the testimony of Jesus.

- receiving God's grace in suffering so we can be taken deeper into Christ.

～～～ 3 ～～～

REDEEMING PAIN

It had been an exhausting year. Our elders approved a sabbatical, and I couldn't wait for it to begin. Then, on a staff-planning retreat I asked an elder about a policy he wasn't observing. He grew silent, turned ice-cold, and responded sharply. I gently pressed him on the issue, and he detonated in anger. His words flew like shrapnel, tearing into me, my wife, and church policy. In an instant, a man I had considered a close friend became an archenemy. Over the next few months, he manipulated others to gain power in the church. A church split seemed inevitable. The betrayal was heart-wrenching.

How do we lead when we are hurt?

CONFRONTING OUR PAIN

While it can be tempting to tuck away our hurt, Paul sets an example by bringing his pain out into the open: "You are aware that all who are in Asia *turned away from me*, among whom are Phygelus and Hermogenes" (2 Timothy 1:15, my italics). He doesn't brush aside his experience; instead, he tells us what people did: "All who are in Asia *turned away from me*" (1:15); "Demas ... has *deserted me*" (4:10); "Alexander ... *did me great harm*" (4:14). In each description he says, *They did it to "me."* These aren't the general pains of ministry: watching a sheep wander off or seeing a marriage crumble. They are *personal*. Real people did real things that hurt Paul. Some of your sufferings are also personal. People have hurt you—some intentionally, others out of neglect, but you bore the brunt. Don't hide these things; acknowledge them. It's ok to admit the hurt. Paul didn't spiritualize the wounds; he confronted them.

Honor the Broken Pieces

Paul also briefly describes what people did to him: betrayal, desertion, great harm. He doesn't wallow in these things, but he does go into some detail. In order for the wounds inflicted from others to heal, it's important to acknowledge what those people have done. When that elder betrayed me, I described the pain in detail to my wife, confided in my mentors, and cried out to God. It can be helpful to talk it out with a spouse, friend, or counselor.

The sting of betrayal is uniquely painful. Although a whole group in Asia "turned away" from Paul, he mentions a couple of names in particular: Phygelus and Hermogenes. The word for "turned away" means "to turn one's back." At one point, Paul's friends were forward-facing brothers-in-arms. But not anymore. I can hear him saying, *We used to be friends, partners in the gospel, but...* The pain of betrayal is unique because it comes from an unlikely, highly trusted source. We expect camaraderie, not treachery, from our friends. The elder who betrayed me had given up personal time to join us in staff meetings, had eaten dinner with us every month, and had even counseled our family through a difficult time. Then he tried to take the church down and lay blame at my feet.

Has someone turned their back on you? A friend, a staff member, a fellow elder? If so, I'm so sorry. I know it hurts. If you haven't spoken about it in detail with someone you trust, I encourage you to do so. Although it may be more painful to open the wound, it will allow God's grace and truth to seep in and heal. Paul was transparent about his hurt. He named it and grieved it. No doubt this letter was tearstained.

After leading through the arduous years of political division, the COVID-19 pandemic, and racial division in 2019–2021, I hit a breaking point. Walking downtown toward our church building one sunny afternoon, something inside of me broke. My heart was suddenly decoupled from the church. A week later I was in an elder meeting telling my friends I couldn't do it anymore. The thought of walking into a room full of church members was harrowing. My emotional reserves were gone. I had no strength for ministry. The elders graciously gave me an impromptu two-month break, during which I frequently broke down in tears. One day I had to pull my car off the road because I couldn't see through the waterfall of tears.

As the days went by, I felt the urge to move past the grief and develop a plan. Something inside of me wanted to justify the time off—to come through with some great insight or repent of some deep sin. But the feeling didn't sit right with my spirit. I was stuck. I went to hear the artist Makoto Fujimura speak on art and faith. He opened by saying, "My entire work can be summarized by two words: 'Jesus wept'." "Oh boy," I thought, "buckle up." Fujimura described God's work in suffering through the process of *kintsugi*. Kintsugi is the Japanese art of bowl-mending.

Artisans reassemble broken tea bowls with costly liquid gold, producing beautiful bowls marked by winding gilt rivulets. Fujimura insists, "They do not fix the bowls; they make them more beautiful." God doesn't just fix us; he beautifies us through suffering.

After Fujimura's talk was over, I turned to my friend and suggested we leave before the Q and A. But we decided to stay. Then, during the Q and A Fujimura's wife, Shim, said, "Makoto, you forgot to mention something important. Before the tea masters begin mending, they hold the pieces in their hands and honor the broken pieces. We have to sit with the broken pieces of our lives and honor them." A lump formed in my throat, and I gasped aloud. This is what God was calling me to do: to honor the broken pieces of my heart. I needed more time to sit with the pain and sorrow.

Jesus took time to honor the brokenness he experienced. He wept. He was "a man of sorrows and acquainted with grief" (Isaiah 53:3). And on the night of his betrayal, he was "sorrowful, even unto death" (Matthew 26:38). Do you need to honor the broken pieces of your life? Perhaps you need to create space to name your pain and grieve beside the man of sorrows? It can be tempting to put up a strong front in ministry, to bury the pain; after all there is so much work to be done. But Paul let his guard down. Jesus wept. We can too.

Entrusting Pain

After we face and grieve our pain, we have to do something with it. Even if we grieve well, hard memories can resurface. Jesus remembered the stinging words of those who had slandered him, "If they have called the master of the house Beelzebul, how much more will they malign those of his household" (Matthew 10:25). It's easy to read over Jesus' pain in an effort to grasp the meaning of his words. But Beelzebul was the name Jews used for the prince of demons, Satan himself (Luke 11:15). His own people accused him of being their archenemy, the architect of death—when Jesus was their deliverer, who had come to give them life!

They totally misjudged Jesus, and people will also misjudge us. This is the point of Jesus' statement. Reasoning from the greater to the lesser, he essentially says, *If they hurl pejoratives at me, the master of the house, how much more will they criticize and name-call those in his house?* While not terribly encouraging, this is true. But there is a grace tucked away in this warning. You are part of Jesus' household. Your persecution is a sign of belonging to the family, and an invitation to know your Master more deeply.

As I grieved my losses, I examined my wounds with the Bible open. Christ met with me personally, profoundly, in Isaiah 53, Lamentations 3, and Psalm 62. It was in the pages of Scripture that I entrusted my sorrows to Jesus. I relinquished them into his care and chose to trust his redemptive plan. As a result, my sufferings became an opportunity for Christ to beautify me. Unaware that I was going to hear Fujimura speak that week, my mom sent me a picture of a kintsugi bowl with the following message: "I see gold all over your life."

Golden lines of grace healed my broken places. God is also mending you with his extravagant grace.

Expecting Pain

It's been said we are always going into suffering, in suffering, or coming out of suffering. That can sound bleak, and it's only part of the picture. There are plenty of joys too. But it is a reminder to expect pain in ministry. How do we avoid becoming hardened by it? Although the accusation against Jesus lodged deeply enough for him to recall it, he didn't stew on the words long enough to become bitter. Instead, he fashioned his accusers' words into a lesson: *Those who follow me will be maligned. Why?* "A disciple is not above his teacher, nor a servant above his master" (Matthew 10:24).

In an age of professionalized ministry, this is an important reminder. We are not above the Lord but below him. We are slaves of a crucified Messiah, not merely strategic leaders or pastor-theologians. However, as Western Christians, we have enjoyed considerable comfort in ministry for generations. We are rarely called the devil, forced to close our churches, or imprisoned for our faith. As a result, it's easy to subtly shift our attention from being a suffering servant to being a visionary leader or a content-creator. It's easy to get consumed with scalable ministry, leadership pipelines, and maximum kingdom impact, or mastery of biblical theology, gospel-centered preaching, and cultural apologetics. While these things have their place, they should not replace our identity as slaves of Christ. Don't try to outplan or outthink your appointed suffering. It's part of your ministry.

I recently heard about a Christian pastor in China who was working with the underground church. Although he was known for promoting kids' programs, serving the poor, a vibrant prayer ministry, and devotion to Jesus, he was accused of sedition against the communist state. One day he was driving home, and four black SUVs surrounded his vehicle. He was forced out of the car and abducted. That was five years ago. His wife and children have not seen him since.

These kinds of accusations and persecutions are not unusual in most of the world, but as our religious freedoms crumble, the conditions for gospel ministry will look more and more like they do elsewhere: like Jesus' ministry. We must ask ourselves: do I see myself mainly as a slave of Christ or as a strategic leader, a pastor theologian, or a content-creator? Being a slave of Christ is better because we are chained to everlasting love. In suffering, we uncover depths of his mysterious love that cannot be found elsewhere. God's love becomes more tangible in sorrow when we entrust our pain to Christ. Our injuries enable us to discover a touch that not only heals our present wound but also radiates outward, touching other broken places and lives. This is love.

ENJOY GOOD GIFTS

It's not all pain and suffering! God also loves to give us good gifts. While Paul acknowledged the hurt inflicted by others, he also recalled the companionship of Timothy, Luke, Mark, Priscilla, Aquila, and Onesiphorus. He spends triple the number of words on Onesiphorus (45 words) than he does on deserters Phygelus and Hermogenes (15 words). *That* is deliberate. We have to choose to see God's goodness; otherwise, we'll veer toward the hard stuff like a car out of alignment.

In the span of a particular week, we had members of ten years' standing drop us an email to say that they were leaving for another church in town, a staff member decide to leave abruptly, a city group report revival-like growth, a counseling session with a couple seeking a divorce after thirty years of marriage, a significant report of gospel advance in Kuala Lumpur through our missionary partners, and a powerful experience of prophetic encouragement directed toward our elders. But because I kept focusing on the difficult stuff, I lost sight of God's goodness. When God convicted me about this, I was freed not only to recognize but relish his goodness! As I recalled each grace, I paused to express gratitude for every one.

How can we cultivate enjoyment of God's gifts? Whenever I get a particularly encouraging email, I don't delete it. Instead, I move it to a special email folder for safekeeping. When I'm tempted to see only the negative things in ministry, I open that folder and scan through the emails, pause, and read one. This practice helps me cherish our church and see God's goodness at work. Paul writes about the specific benefits of his companionship with Onesiphorus: *He often refreshed me, was not ashamed of my chains, searched for me earnestly, and found me.* Observations like that don't just fall onto us; they require deliberate reflection on God's grace.

Many of us in ministry find it difficult to enjoy God's gifts. We can be so driven by principle—doing things for the kingdom—that we fail to enjoy the gifts of our King. When I am given some time off, I typically wrestle for a couple days with a condemning voice telling me that I don't deserve it. The voice reminds me that others are working while I am resting. The accuser is intent on poisoning God's good gifts of rest and play with condemning words, but our Advocate reminds us of how much our heavenly Father loves to give us good things, "If you then, who are evil, know how to give good gifts to your children, how much more will your Father who is in heaven give good things to those who ask him!" (Matthew 7:11). The key to enjoying God's gifts is to receive them like a child. Children don't refuse or reluctantly receive gifts. They don't think of themselves as worthy or undeserving. They receive them with great joy and plead with their parents for more! This is how we should receive from our generous Father. So, enjoy that break, go to the movies with that friend, and delight in the gifts God gives you, without a hint of guilt. God delights in your enjoyment of his gifts, just as you delight in your children tearing open a present on Christmas morning.

When we take time to reflect on the good gifts God has given us, it compounds the grace we have received. Do you have a practice of relishing God's gifts? Do you set aside time to reflect on how God has blessed you through your church? If not, consider dedicating an electronic note to this, updating it as you go. Make a habit of asking others, "Where are you seeing God's goodness these days?" Consider journaling with an eye on his graces. Take your observations to God in prayers of gratitude and praise. Your heart will sing!

STRENGTH TO KEEP GOING

The practice of cherishing God's grace is tested when we experience frequent turnover in our ministry. College students graduate every four or so years; busy urbanites take jobs in other cities; young couples mature into families and move into the suburbs. We've had five different churches in 13 years, and they've all been City Life Church.

Although transience is a feature of ministry in modern America, it's also something Paul was familiar with. At the end of 2 Timothy, Paul relates the comings and goings of many partners in the gospel. People come and people go—something Timothy also sees in Ephesus. As Paul sits alone in his cell, he writes, "You then, my child, be strengthened by the grace that is in Christ Jesus" (2 Timothy 2:21). Because people come and go, we must draw strength from the one who doesn't leave, disappoint, or abandon us.

One obstacle to operating out of God's strength is that we tend to operate from different strengths. Some leaders lean on their strategic plans: "If I execute the right plan and get people into this system, then ministry will hum." Others glide by on their winsome personality: "If I stay connected with people and make sure they know I love them, no one will wander off." Many put faith in their facility for teaching the Scriptures: "If I just preach the gospel and ground people in the Word of God, they won't cause division." But the strength required for ministry comes from outside of us, not within us. The vigor to endure comings and goings comes from the grace that is *in Christ Jesus.*

Union with Christ
The phrase "in Christ" refers to our *union with Christ.* When we put our faith in Jesus, we are placed into Jesus, united with him in inseparable, mystical union. In many respects, the Christian life is about settling into this blessed union. It is in this intimate relationship that

we enjoy his grace: redemptive forgiveness, justified acceptance, heavenly intercession, adoptive love, and new-creation identity. This is so central to Christianity that the phrase *in Christ* occurs over 100 times in Paul's letters alone. Christ is also in us.

When I was living in Volgograd, Russia, for a summer, I bought several Russian *matryoshka* dolls as souvenir gifts. These wooden dolls nest inside one another. Perhaps it's helpful to think of our union with Jesus as three identical versions of such a doll: large, medium, and small.

Since Jesus is bigger than us, we are placed inside of him. We are hidden with Christ in God (Colossians 3:3). The enveloping presence of God is what defines us most. It is where we are most secure, most loved, most satisfied. But if we are opened up, there is also a "smaller version" of Christ inside of us. Christ is also in us: "I am in my Father, and you in me, *and I in you*" (emphasis added, John 14:20). Bafflingly, Jesus indwells us.[20] His presence enables us to be the truest, purest version of ourselves. He purifies our motives, strengthens our resolve, and together with the Holy Spirit transforms us. Enjoying this union with Christ enables us to absorb his strength and enjoy his grace.

We are like the middle matryoshka doll, and God wants us to reflect Jesus within our own dimensions; to be the *Christified* version of ourselves. This means resting in Jesus' surrounding outer presence: walk in what he thinks of you; believe his words about you. You are his. It also means cherishing the indwelling Son of God, who strengthens our inner self, which is being renewed day by day (2 Corinthians 4:16) and sheds abroad his love in our hearts through the Holy Spirit (Romans 5:5). He is "Christ in you, the hope of glory," giving witness to a future free of sin, sorrow, and heartache—one filled with joy and peace (Colossians 1:27). We are in Christ and Christ is in us.

We are wonderfully designed to operate *in* Jesus' enveloping strength and according to Jesus' intimate love. With Christ without and Christ within, we have everything necessary to endure ministry turmoil. The very Son of God is with us, in us, and around us, everywhere we go. As Paul says, "All [things] are yours, and you are Christ's, and Christ is God's" (2 Corinthians 3:22-23). What more could we need?!

Gospel Dynamic in Ministry

How does union with Jesus affect ministry? Union with Christ generates a *gospel dynamic* in our leadership: when we relate to others out of union with Christ, there is strength to lead. But when we relate to people out of our own strength, we're drained by the demands of leadership. For years, one of my daughters would wake up in an awful mood. She wouldn't respond to our questions or instructions. Instead, she moped about making everyone late to school or work. When I was mindful of my union with Christ, I had much more patience with her struggles. But when I operated out of my strength, I was easily frustrated and quick to make a cutting remark. The same is true in ministry.

There is a noticeable difference in my energy for service to the church when I am experiencing Christ in solitude, prayer, and meditation. This daily retreat into his presence strengthens me for the day ahead. The enjoyment of Christ is mystical but tied to truth about Christ. So, when reading Scripture, I look for what the passage tells me about God and latch on to that, ruminate on it, and turn it into conversational prayer with Jesus. Once I have a word from Christ, I go for a walk.

During my walk I begin by responding to my surroundings. I thank God for the quiet, the chirping birds, the fresh cool air, the bright sunshine, the beautiful flowers. My surroundings point me to the artistic Creator and sovereign Sustainer of all things. This leads me into more personal conversation with him, which is especially invigorating. When I pray aloud, my heart is drawn to God as though he is a person, which helps me dwell in Christ as he abides in me. These simple, sweet times give me spiritual energy for the day.

They also give me something to come back to throughout the day. Recently, I was meditating on Ephesians 1 and was struck by how I often live as though I *do not* have every spiritual blessing in Christ Jesus. But I do! When tempted to complain, I was drawn back to this profound reality: God has not held back from me but has given me *every* spiritual blessing in the heavenly places *in Christ Jesus* (Ephesians 1:3). He is lavish and good. We have all we need in Jesus.

GRACE WORKS

It's often been said that grace is opposed to earning but not to effort. In order for our churches and organizations to flourish, we must work hard and well. Grace works.

Images of Ministry Faithfulness

Paul uses three figures to demonstrate the faithfulness required for ministry: those of soldier, athlete, and farmer (2 Timothy 2:3-6).[21] All three work hard and according to the rules of their vocation. A farmer toils to till the soil. A good soldier strives to please his commanding officer. An athlete disciplines himself to win. In the Greek games, athletes had to take a vow before a statue of Zeus, promising that they had trained for ten months and had been faithful in diet, discipline, and exercise.[22]

Lance Armstrong won seven consecutive Tour de France titles, elevated the popularity of cycling to global status, and contributed hundreds of millions of dollars to cancer research through his non-profit Livestrong. He was an outspoken, brash victor, known for his gloating. But after he was exposed for doping, his titles were stripped, his character tarnished, and his non-profit struggled. Annual donations plummeted from $40 million in 2009 to $2.5 million in 2018.

Shortly after Armstrong was banned for life from competitive cycling, I sat down to eat lunch with a friend. He whispered, "Look to your right." As I nonchalantly looked over my shoulder, I noticed Lance sitting next to me with his cap pulled down and clothes disheveled, speaking quietly. He clearly wanted to avoid attention. If we don't serve the Lord according to his holy rules, we risk being banned from vocational ministry, or worse.

It can be enticing to reach for something other than Jesus to get through the rough patches. Some leaders overeat. Others become detached and inaccessible. Posting online replaces prayer. Meeting with other pastors replaces pastoral care. Some leaders reach for alcohol to "wind down" from the demands of leadership. Dependence upon anything other than Jesus will lead to failure and bring ruin upon our ministries. An athlete is only crowned if he competes according to the rules. The reward is great—eternity with Christ and his people in his new creation—but so is the loss.

Labor for the Reward

Why endure it all? For the reward! All three of these figures have something else in common. *They work for the reward.* The soldier serves for the prize of pleasing his commanding officer. The athlete competes to obtain the crown, and the farmer works for the pleasure of sinking his teeth into homegrown fruit. Our God is a rewarder of those who seek him (Hebrews 11:6).

Enjoy the reward of your calling! Preach your heart out on Sundays. Celebrate new Christians through baptism. Revel in Jesus's presence and forgiveness during communion. Delight in discipling new believers. Enjoy sharing the gospel with non-Christians. Marvel as leaders take the reins of ministry. Rejoice when you see the poor lifted up and justice for victims of injustice. Capture these rewarding moments and trace their glint to your future crown, an emblem of endless reward where we will enjoy the undying favor of Jesus and the perfect love of his people, in God's new creation.

THE UNWAVERING PASTOR

An unwavering pastor perseveres through pain by:

- talking transparently about pain with others.

- allowing pain to help us identify as slaves of Christ

- looking for and enjoying the good gifts of God.

- prioritizing union with Christ over personal strengths.

- working for the reward.

～4～
DIVISIVE WORDS

Eileen was magnetic.[23] People were drawn to her humor and fun-loving personality. She hosted folks in her home every week and encouraged them in the faith. Community thickened in her wake. But after she invested herself into a noble cause, she began to repel people. A subversive spirit grew among her followers. Eventually her discontent boiled over into an arduous year of meetings with church leaders. One by one, those in Eileen's circle slowly broke away from the church, dismembering the congregation. Their weapon? Words.

WORD-FIGHTING

Words can wound, and words can heal. Solomon writes, "There is one whose rash words are like sword thrusts, but the tongue of the wise brings healing" (Proverbs 12:18). It can be difficult to recover from repeated jabs. In our first few years of marriage, my wife and I got into awful arguments that lasted hours. She would say that something I said or did hurt her, and instead of empathizing with her, I would interject a justification, remarking how it hurt me that she would think I would do something to hurt her! She would reply by saying, "That's not what I said."

I would say, "Yes you did."

Around and around we went, until my wife would despairingly cry out, "I don't even know what we're talking about anymore!" I had lost the forest for the trees, and almost lost my wife.

Paul warns churches about this kind of quarrel, "Charge them before God not to quarrel about words, which does no good, but only ruins the hearers" (2 Timothy 2:14). He coins a term to get his point across—*word-fighting*—a compound word comprising *logos* (word) and *machomai* (to engage in physical combat). Avoiding fighting words is in our best interest. But if we aren't supposed to fight with words, how are we supposed to work through our differences? Paul isn't saying don't differ *with* words; he's saying don't fight *about* words. Don't nitpick over one another's vocabulary. Listen with a charitable spirit.

After I had preached one Sunday, Eileen texted me to express concern about my use of the phrase "cognitive minority." She was offended that I had used the word "minority" without giving adequate attention to ethnic minorities. To be sure, the word can be used insensitively or to discriminate; however, I wasn't addressing racial issues. I had used the sociological term "cognitive minority", to encourage the church to suffer well when their biblical views are diminished by broader cultural views. As a faithful "gospel minority", we shouldn't surrender our convictions to liberal or conservative thinking.

Unfortunately, Eileen fixated on the word "minority" and isolated it from its context. I listened to better understand where she was coming from and affirmed her concern for minorities. Yet, as our discussion continued, it became clear that her cultural lexicon was more important than my intended meaning or the biblical context of the sermon. This posture toward sermons became a trend: listening for certain phrases or references to current events instead of cherishing the intended biblical or homiletical meaning.

Paul warns that these quarrels can *ruin* the listeners: a word that can also be translated "destroy." As Eileen continued to prioritize her cultural views over Scripture, she shared her contentions with friends, souring their view of church leaders. As a result, her ungracious criticism spread, straining relationships, sowing discord, and stimulating distrust of church leaders. Eventually, most of the people in her circle left the church. Word-fighting had led to ruin.

Consider for a moment how God responds to our words about him. While he has given us the Scriptures as an inerrant guide, he has accommodated our error and imprecision for millennia. I have held wrong views about creation and salvation—even about his Spirit and his Son—and yet I have never felt condemned by him. When our theology is off, lightening doesn't strike. God is patient. He knows our theology and faith are worked out over time. What if we practiced the same kind of patient generosity toward one another? What if we heeded Jesus' instruction to pay attention to the log in our own eyes instead of fixating on the speck in the eyes of others?

Of course, there are times for correction. But when God corrects us through the consistent witness of Scripture and knowledgeable teachers, he does so with a heart of love. We often pounce on one another with hard hearts and feeble understanding. What if Christians adopted a disposition of love when offended: covering a multitude of sins, keeping no record of wrongs, bearing all things, believing all things, hoping all things, enduring all things? We could move toward constructive peacemaking instead of destructive ruin.

Word-fighting often leads to dissension, slander, and evil suspicion (1 Timothy 6:4). Our leaders bore the brunt of backdoor slander and pervasive mistrust, which led to dissension. These conflicts wear pastors out, draining them of emotional, physical, and spiritual energy. Paul is right: word-fighting does no good. Worse, it can split a church. But love builds it up, making the church a community that assumes the best of others, extends the benefit of the doubt, and disagrees charitably. Like my marital arguments, word-fighting has the power to destroy relationships.

LEADING THROUGH CONTROVERSY

If Christians are to avoid fighting about words, should we avoid controversy altogether? Paul argued frequently with Greek and Roman philosophers in the *agora*, with Jewish experts in the synagogues, and with Christians in their churches. He was known to "debate": a word used positively of his argument in an exchange described as "no small dissension" (Acts 15:1-2). Paul addressed controversy head on, much like his Savior. Jesus debated religious leaders publicly and challenged everyone's thinking. He was criticized by conservative Pharisees and progressive Sadducees. Jesus was a controversialist.[24] Similarly, pastors are called to model healthy debate while avoiding an "unhealthy craving for controversy" (1 Timothy 6:4).

Controversy is more than a misunderstanding between people. It erupts when two parties are staunchly at odds. While some truth may be debated, the discord that swells often overtakes the truth. Unhealthy craving kicks in when people become more passionate about being right than being respectful and more interested in winning than loving. As a result, they justify hateful speech and unkind action.

Spiritual deceit is behind a lot of controversy. Our true foe is not an opposing political party nor is it one another. Our enemy is Satan. Our family is the Church. We battle not against flesh and blood but against principalities and powers. While not exhaustive, here are a few principles to keep in mind in the midst of controversy.

Pray, Pray, Pray

We can become so embroiled in the details of a controversy that we lose sight of the broader spiritual war. When I was unjustly attacked by an elder, it was easy to get bogged down in his accusations. Am I really unfit for ministry? Do I deserve his anger? While self-reflection is important, the enemy prefers to trap us here. It took some time for me to realize that our conflict wasn't based on a misunderstanding but a spiritually provoked controversy. Then, I began to really pray.

As we prayed, the fog began to lift. People swept away by the elder's deceit began to see what was happening. After seeing the controversy not as a personality conflict but a spiritual provocation, a staff member confided, "When I looked at him I saw darkness, but when I looked at you I saw light." When controversy erupts, reach for your spiritual armor and pray without ceasing. Pray against the enemy and for your opponents. Pray for a tender heart and a strong spirit. Pray for humility and grace to endure. Pray for the glory of God.

Listen Well

As a young leader, I had a hard time receiving any kind of critique. I felt that I had the theological answers, and it was everybody else's job to agree. After all, I was trying to be faithful to Scripture (though my reading was selective!). As a result, I misinterpreted questions as lack of support. I did not listen well. Instead, when I sensed that a staff member was struggling to grasp our vision, I interrupted to steer them in the right direction. Eventually frustration boiled over during a team exercise.

A staff member shared that when I cut him off, he felt disrespected. I had no idea. Seeing the answer more clearly, I thought I was doing him a favor by efficiently guiding him to the right conclusion. He explained that allowing him to process and ask questions enabled him to truly own a conclusion, instead of having it handed to him. A light bulb went on. I apologized and made a conscious effort not to interrupt my staff.

Sometimes we have to walk *with people* all the way around the barn to get to the front door. Otherwise, they might not actually go in. They need space to come to some conclusions. Now, sometimes people just need to do their job; not everything is up for debate, but if we don't listen well, people may nod their head in agreement while internalizing frustration. A good leader listens to others even if it feels inefficient, because love is inefficient. Jesus could have snapped his fingers and been done with creation, redemption, history—the whole thing—but instead he threw efficiency to the wind and wastefully entered our mess to bring about new creation. Listen well and you will love well.

Affirm What's Right

As we listen to others, it is important to take note of the things that are correct. Conflict is a two-way street designed for mutual change. God wants to transform us into the image of his Son in the thick of controversy. When we hear things that are true and good, we should affirm them. If we hear something that convicts us, we should apologize and repent. If we need time to consider something further, we should voice that need, making sure to follow up after we have had time to think and pray. Honor what is good and right, regardless of the source. Grant dignity to those who oppose you.

Filter through the Spirit

Controversy easily overtakes those who listen *defensively*. The defensive person listens long enough to gather ammunition to make their case. Their aim is to be proven right. We can also fuel controversy by listening *compliantly*. The compliant person listens without speaking the truth. Their aim is to be accepted, even if it requires a white lie or a snub of the Spirit. Instead, of being defensive or compliant, filter everything through the Holy Spirit.

The godly leader practices double-listening: listening to the person and to the Spirit. As you listen, filter what is said through Scripture, noting any incongruence. This is where the Spirit speaks most clearly. As you weigh areas of concern, ask the Spirit for discernment on what to address. Remember to be patient with evil and to correct your opponents with gentleness. When you need to correct, try to avoid correcting based on your general spiritual opinion. Instead, appeal to your shared authority in Scripture. Filter what is said through the Spirit.

Know What You're Walking Into

I have walked into too many meetings that turned out to be an ambush. If a critical person asks for a meeting, don't be afraid to ask them what they want to meet about. This enables us to think and pray over a topic instead of walking into a meeting as if blindfolded. It is also wise to ask a fellow leader or pastor to join you. This increases prayer and includes a witness should anything go sideways. Once you meet in person, ask the individual what they want out of the meeting. This gets the real agenda on the table and helps avoid word-fighting.

Dr. David Smith oversees 250 churches in our metro area. He has led many of them through church conflict. When I invited him to mediate a conflict with a hostile church member, he asked me what the church member wanted. I had no idea. "This," he said, "is your first step." When he met with a group to field charges against me, the first question he asked was "What do you want out of this meeting?" When it became clear that someone wanted me to step down, David said, "Is this for a moral, ethical, legal, or biblical reason?" They admitted they had none of those reasons. David's initial penetrating question exposed an unbiblical agenda, which led to my vindication. The controversy was driven by a thirst for power. It can be extremely helpful to know what we're walking into.

It's also wise to invite people to pray at the outset of a controversial meeting to ask God for mutual humility, patience, wisdom, and grace. If they refuse or resist prayer, it can be a sign they aren't ready to resolve conflict. So, pray at the beginning, throughout, and at the end of the meeting: *Lord, help us!*

Stay Close to Jesus

It is so important to stay close to Jesus during controversy. When we are close to him, we enjoy his sympathetic heart for sufferers. He is close to the downcast and the brokenhearted. Intimacy with Christ also keeps us humble and open to the transformative work God wants to do in us. When we are close to Jesus, his words are louder than our critics' words. We are reminded that we are his disciple before we are a leader; we are the Father's beloved son or daughter prior to being a pastor. This frees us to heed fair critiques without being devastated, and to dismiss unjust charges without being embittered.

IRREVERENT BABBLE

Just because we apply these biblical principles in controversy doesn't mean things will turn out peachy. Often, things get worse before they get better. Once Satan's attack is exposed, he often tries a different tactic. Fighting words may devolve into what Paul describes as "irreverent babble," which affects more people and spreads like gangrene (2 Timothy 2:16–17).

Gangrene presents as discoloration in body parts caused by lack of blood supply. It can lead to body-wide sepsis and even death. An irreverent babbler threatens the community with their unfiltered speech. This is the person who goes on and on about the bad qualities or decisions of others. They are intoxicated with their own perspective and have very little reverence for those in positions of authority. They troll (or trawl) social-media feeds for certain words, censure sermons for specific phrases, listen with a judgmental lexicon, and eagerly correct or call out others. Their speech is like many sword thrusts. Paul says, "avoid irreverent babble." Don't entertain it. Unfollow, disassociate, rebuke.

Irreverent babble surfaced with Eileen. She stopped encouraging her leaders and even spoke condescendingly to them. When the elders met with her to appeal for more godly speech, we were told not to pull a "Jesus juke."[25] She trivialized Jesus. It was her way or the highway. When we gently tried to correct her for gossip and subversion, she accused us of sexism. When she departed, the church was left to pick up relational pieces in the wake of her false worship.

Looking back, the elders should have called her out much sooner. We wanted to listen well and filter through the Spirit, but we were tolerating a body-threatening disease. Irreverent babblers must be called out sooner than later, for the good of the church. If you lengthen the fuse, the bomb still goes off. When you hear fighting words, irreverent babble, and disregard for church authority, don't wait. Charge people like this to repent of their sin and return to Jesus. Appeal to Christ's authority, not your own, and speak the truth in love.

If you struggle to speak with warm-fuzzies in your heart, that is ok. A leader must defend his people, chase down the wandering sheep, and ward off wolves, especially when it's hard. When Jesus rebuked Peter, he wasn't doing back-flips inside. When Peter confronted Ananias and Sapphira, it was with a broken heart: "Why have you contrived this deed in your heart? You have not lied to man but God" (Acts 5:4.) But Peter learned from Jesus how important it is for the love of the church to expose idolatry.

LEADING WITH GOD'S WORDS

While it is important to consider how *not* to use words, it is even more important to know how to *use* words. Paul's solution to fighting words isn't merely to correct but to handle God's words like a workman: "Do your best to present yourself to God as one approved, a worker who has no need to be ashamed, rightly handling the word of truth" (2 Timothy 2:15). This command is sandwiched between the exhortations about quarrelers and babblers—a reminder to rely on the word of God as we shepherd. The word is our work, not best practices or strategic outcomes. But the Bible is not a puzzle to solve or an apologetic handbook to consult; it is divine speech to interpret and heed. "Do your best," Paul says, which means to be "zealously observant."

Are you zealously observant in how you handle God's word? Would your exegesis pass God's test? Or do you depend too heavily on secondary sources, borrow from other preachers, or copy other leaders' techniques? Depending on your gifting, you may be more zealous about your new strategy, program, or pet theology, but when we stand before God to give an account for our ministry, he won't ask about our strategies, programs, or insights. He'll want to know how we handled his word for his people.

How do we handle God's word? Rightly. The word means "to cut straight." To cut a board straight, it must be cut correctly. Before we moved into a new house, we hired a carpenter to build a mantel for the fireplace. When I inspected it, I noticed a gap between the mantel and the wall. The mantel wasn't quite flush with the Sheetrock. Assuming the carpenter hadn't cut the board correctly, I pointed out the gap to him. He replied, "The wall is crooked." I thought he was joking! But he explained how he always cuts his boards straight, and that walls are often uneven. The unashamed workman strives to cut the word straight, and when he does, the Bible exposes gaps in our lives.

To cut the word straight, we must strive to honor the intent of the biblical author. What is Jesus, Paul, or Moses trying to say? Often we come to a text with our own goals or expectations. Seeking encouragement, we may distort a convicting psalm into a warm fuzzy. Working with an assumption about how God views race, sex, or gender, we may read that assumption into the text. Eager to address an issue, we may distort the Bible to get a felt-need point across. But Paul says the way to lead through controversy is by honoring the author's intent. Our task is to read the intended meaning out of the text and into the lives of the people we pastor.

It is also important to teach others to do the same. When they have an issue that is at odds with the Bible, teach them to respect the divine Author over the fallible interpreter: to hold God's views higher than their opinions. Work with the Bible until the truth comes out. Honor the author's intent and plead with the Spirit to put it in the church.

We should handle the word with zeal to pass God's test, not the scrutiny of our church or culture. To do this we must study carefully, plead for the Spirit's insight into his words, and ask him to deconstruct our invisible agendas. We do this so we can make his intention for his people crystal clear: to close the gaps. If we cut the word straight, we can be assured God will do his work. Sometimes we get to see people more flush with Christ. At other times people will reject or distort his word. Either way, if we're faithful to God's words, we can entrust the results to him.

ALLOWING THE GOSPEL TO LEAD YOU

In times of division it is critical for leaders and their churches to lean into union with Christ. Otherwise, we will be pulled apart. Anticipating the need to do this, Paul says, "Remind them of these things" prior to his charge to not word-fight (2 Timothy 2:14). The "these things" is a grounding, poetic reminder of the gospel (2 Timothy 2:11-13):

If we have died with him,
we will also live with him;
if we endure,
we will also reign with him;
if we deny him,
he also will deny us;
if we are faithless,
he remains faithful—
for he cannot deny himself.

Paul's use of poetry evokes a memorable reflection on the beauty of a life lived with Christ. The first, superdense line reminds us that if we have died with Christ—to sin, death, and hell—we will also live with Christ—in righteousness, resurrection, and the new creation. Our past-tense death inevitably leads to a glorious future life with Christ. This future life is "already" and "not fully." We already possess new life in Christ, which enables us to patiently lead through controversial circumstances. But our impatience with others also reminds us that the new life is not fully realized. When we are worn thin, it is hopeful to remember that inexhaustible life is coming.

The eschatological overtones of the first line carry over into the second line: if we endure, we will also reign with him. The reward of our endurance is shocking—we will rule over God's new creation with the Lord of all, "The one who conquers, I will grant him to sit with me on my throne" (Revelation 3:21). This dignifying promise is a comforting thought when we are snubbed or mocked. Keep going, pastor! Chin up, leader! Regardless of what others think, Jesus thinks so highly of you that he will put you on his throne! Reigning from his lap! This reward is not only for leaders. In Christ's new creation, every struggling saint will catch up to their new life in Christ, flush with his virtues in a revamped creation.

The cost of abandoning Christ, however, is terrifying: he will deny us. Jesus says to those who loved ministry more than him, "I never knew you; depart from me" (Matthew 7:21-23). Yet he also pledges to be faithful when we are faithless. What is the difference between faithlessness and denial? The faithless lapse in trusting Christ, but the deniers turn their back on him. Although the faithless stumble through pelting hail, they persevere with Christ.

In culturally polarizing times, it can be tempting to find comfort in a partisan Christ who will place a halo over our politics. But the biblical Jesus calls us to renounce the world and follow him—to allow the gospel to lead us.

And when we are faithless, he is faithful. Why? He cannot deny himself. Christ's faithfulness to us is grounded in his ontology. New Testament scholar Gordon Fee comments, "To be unfaithful to us would mean God had ceased to be." [26] Jesus cannot un-be, for he is the I AM. God is essentially, covenantally, bound to his people in tremendous undying love. Flush with the perfect pledge of God's covenantal love, we have theft-proof resources to love a broken and often belligerent world.

THE UNWAVERING PASTOR

An unwavering pastor engages in controversy by:

- avoiding word-fighting and correcting babblers.

- leading through controversy by praying, listening, affirming, and filtering.

- correcting people with God's word, not personal opinion.

- cutting the word straight and letting it do the work.

~~~ 5 ~~~

AGE OF THE SELF

Having hurtled through space and time in an unreliable Tardis, Doctor Who and companion land on an unknown planet.[27] As the Doctor opens the Tardis door, the companion steps out and asks, "When are we?" Although we don't yet travel interdimensional space, this question is among the most important we can ask. There are two answers to this question—When are we?—that, if grasped, unlock wisdom and power for ministry. The first answer orients us to when we are *theologically*. Paul says we're in the last days. The second answer orients us to when are we *culturally*: in the age of self. How do we lead in the last days, which are stained with the love of self?

THE LAST DAYS

If we really are in the last days, shouldn't we have been notified of the imminent impact of a massive asteroid? Perhaps we should be witnessing spontaneous raptures and vacant cars violently colliding into one another. Or maybe an Elijah sighting. What is the sign of the last days? Paul writes, "But understand this, that *in the last days* there will come times of difficulty" (2 Timothy 3:1, my italics). The word *chalepos* means troublesome, difficult times of stress. Intense stress is a sign of the times.

A 2020 poll taken by the American Psychiatric Association reports that 62 percent of Americans felt more anxious than the year before, a figure nearly double the anxiety levels of each of the previous three years.[28] Reasons cited include concern over the coronavirus, gun violence, politics, financial instability, and climate-change impact. Our consciences are hard pressed by difficult questions: Am I anti-racist? Will I get COVID? Who should I vote for? Is war coming? This is a lot to live through and even more to lead through!

But the last days are also marked by something gloriously positive. At Pentecost Peter announced, *"And in the last days* it shall be, God declares, that I will pour out my Spirit on all flesh"* (Acts 2:17; quoting Joel 2:28). The outpouring of God's Spirit upon all peoples, not just the occasional Old Testament prophet, was a sign the last days had begun. The end times are marked by an outpouring of the Spirit.

It's hard for us to conceive of "the last days" stretching out from the 1st century to the 21st century, but that's because we put chronology before theology. When we hear the term, we often think *numerically*—how many days left until the end of the world or before Jesus comes back? But the Bible thinks *redemptively*—how are things different now that Jesus has come? The Bible tells time on a gospel clock. When Jesus ascended to the right hand of the Father, testifying to our redemption, the Spirit descended to launch us into redemptive witness of his love for the world. The last days, though centuries long and anxiety-filled, are a precious time for gospel witness in the Spirit's power.

SELF-LOVE

A pastor who walks in the Spirit experiences life and peace (Romans 8:6), but a leader who fixates on adversity is filled with exhaustion and worry. How we cope with adversity either feeds the Spirit or awakens the flesh. In 2020, alcohol sales doubled, viewing and downloading of porn skyrocketed,[29] and calls to suicide hotlines jumped by 1,000 percent.[30] The coping mechanisms that we keep a lid on in good times will, in hard times, blow the lid off.

During the weeks of pandemic lockdown I found myself surfing the web for shoes while I lay in bed at night. I even waited for a pair to "drop," snapping up a pair of Air Jordan 1s before they sold out. Although I liked shoes before lockdown, the like became a love in difficult times. Instead of scrolling through God's graces from the day as I lay in bed, I scrolled sneaker sites. It was my attempt to cope with the oppressive conditions—an escape—and it didn't work. I quickly found out that a pair of sneakers doesn't dissolve anxiety; it only delays it.

In 2 Timothy 3, Paul lists 18 carnal ways of coping, ranging from arrogance to not loving goodness. We could examine each vice in detail, but they all fit neatly under one heading: *lovers of self* (v 2). This phrase is actually one Greek word, *philautos*, which combines a word for love with the word for oneself—self-love. If we cleared away the coping mechanisms and peeled back all our anxieties, at the bottom of our hearts we would find a pool of turbid self-love.

When we love ourselves, we're drawn to things that serve us, like money and the comfort it affords. Tumbling down the hole of self-love, we fall for the idea that we deserve certain treatment or things, and that self-preoccupation numbs us to the needs of others. During lockdown, I began to see my children as an impediment to work, disgruntled church members as an inconvenience, and even my wife as an obstruction to escape. Some nights I lay in bed talking to my wife when what I really wanted to do was to zone out on Netflix. As restaurant owners struggled to return from pandemic conditions, owners in San Francisco reported customers yelling, demanding, and leaving scathing reviews.[31] Many of us became so self-focused during lockdown that we emerged seeing people as obstacles to comfort, not objects of love or respect.

When self-love is prioritized above the church, ministry becomes a drag. We come dangerously close to "having the appearance of godliness but denying its power" (3:5). We settle for a veneer of holiness while lusting for the praise of men. We also deny the power of godliness when we are passionate about politics or justice but heartless and unjust to those who don't see things the way we do. We cave in to the love of self when we speak harshly, not compassionately, about the church member caught in sin. We may look godly on the outside—attending church, participating in small group, pursuing justice, preaching the gospel, and tithing ten percent—while indifferent to Christ's heart for sinners. When we choose self-love, we live more in the cultural moment than in the redemptive-historical age. Instead of settling for a veneer of Christianity, we need to dive deeply into Christ and bring others along with us. But to do that, it is helpful to know the strain of self-love we are dealing with.

THE CULT OF FEELING

The band Walk the Moon sings, "I am my own sanctuary ... hero ... teacher ... best friend ... Friday night ... my own love of my life."[32] This is the reigning cultural mantra: you do you. Our society worships at the altar of self; the object of devotion is feelings. We assign divinity-level status to ourselves, expecting others to affirm whatever we feel. Ethicist Alistair McIntyre calls our feeling-based ethic *emotivism,* in which "all morals are nothing but expressions of preference ... expressions of attitudes or feelings."[33] Emotivism invites moral calamity: "I feel more male than female." "I feel like whites are superior to blacks." "I long for the same-sex."

When we embrace emotivism, moralities proliferate, producing endless conflict. The ensuing clash of tribal emotions produces what McIntyre calls the *interminable character* of moral disagreements. These disagreements, which we view publicly on social media, are interminable not in the sense that the arguments go on and on, although they sometimes do, but in the sense that *they can find no terminus*—no shared end point from which to determine what is right or wrong. As a result, conflicts over what is just cannot be solved and escalate into shouting matches. Whoever shouts the loudest, posts the longest, or garners the greatest sympathy wins.

When emotivism seeps into the church, it often divides God's people into groups based on preferences. These groups can become so feelings focused that they displace our uniting authority—God's word and his gospel of grace. The "gospel of preference" takes its place, empowering groups or individuals to criticize leaders for not aligning with their preference. In my experience, and the experience of many pastors I speak with, emotivist Christians foist a particular course of action upon the church, requiring them to comply with their passion. But if we complied with every request, Sunday mornings would devolve into a PR session for pet causes.

This ethical pragmatism aligns with the critique of philosopher Charles Taylor, focusing "on defining the *content of obligation* rather than the *nature of the good life*; and it has no conceptual place left for a notion of the good as the object of our love or allegiance" (emphasis added).[34] The content of obligation, determined by an individual or group, becomes more important than the nature of the good. People become so focused on *doing good* that they lose sight of *what good is*.

As a result, they make anger-fueled demands: *Why didn't you announce that shooting? You need to tell the church to protest. I'm not coming to church unless everyone wears a mask! Wearing masks is Biden-worship. You need to get our church to sign up for a whiteness intensive. If you cared about adoption, you would host this seminar.* The Beatitudes (Matthew 5:2-11) become optional, and the latest political checklist becomes essential. Christians insist on their new vision of the good in very unvirtuous ways. Without a shared objective basis from which to determine the good, such Christians are bound to war with others in the church. A cult of feeling is hatched within the church, and we are sidetracked from Christ.

However, the church is called to gather around the risen Christ, not individual causes. This does not mean we should avoid addressing injustices such as racial injustice, abuse of spiritual authority, gender oppression, xenophobia and homophobia. It does mean that we must subordinate our personal passions for various causes to the person of Christ. Instead of being transfixed by a particular cause and holding church leaders hostage to a supposed best practice, Christians should examine how Scripture speaks to issues, instructs us to relate to our leaders, and allows for a diversity of approaches in mission, while charitably pursuing a Christ-centered ethic together. Christians are in a unique position to champion the true nature of the good from Scripture and express it in our speech, thoughts, and actions.

LEADING EMOTIVIST CHRISTIANS

When Christians privilege other sources of authority over Scripture and local-church leadership, they begin to drift from their community. Newfound insights can be electrifying and, if not submitted to the sieve of Scripture, produce elitism. This elitism displaces the humble character of Jesus, giving the individual a sense of self-righteous exceptionalism. As a result, they begin to spend more time with like-minded people, whether online or in person. Excarnational networks begin to displace incarnational commitments. Ideological affinity can create the feeling of community without its substance. Slowly church commitments become optional as shared exceptionalism leads people to withdraw from communities who challenge their newfound beliefs. Small groups or even entire churches must be converted to the individual's viewpoint or abandoned.

Emotivist Christians approach relationships with a "join or die" mentality; brothers and sisters in Christ are reduced to potential converts or collateral damage. This sounds intentionally sinister, but often the shift happens slowly and unconsciously. People are often unaware that they have been radicalized by strong left- or right-wing ideas. But before they know it, they have ghosted friends, abandoned communities, and gossiped about leaders to justify a new trajectory that privileges their newfound authority. Leaders have to pick up the pieces.

How should pastors respond to emotivism in their churches? Is Scripture too antiquated to help us lead through these modern dilemmas? While terms and theories often change, sins and strategies of Satan remain the same.

Expose Emotivism Before the Church

Ignoring emotivism is an inadequate response. It is imperative that Christian leaders name this pervasive idolatry of self before the church. In the 1st century, Timothy was called to confront individuals who crept into homes and captured women burdened by sins, and led them astray into passions (3:6). In the 21st century, these "individuals" creep into every home, through every screen, baiting every heart. Enemies come under the cover of data, appealing to sensitive consciences through impassioned testimonies and online "conversations."

We should preach, teach, and counsel on the dangers of emotivism, but do so from the inspired authority of Scripture. In the end, any appeal through cultural critique will be rebutted by another cultural source. We must elevate the authority of Scripture, helping others to see that, where applicable, their debate is not with their leaders or churches but with God himself. We must commend Jesus' beatitudinal vision of the good and implore the church to reflect his vision in how they interact with one another.[35]

Present a Biblical View of Emotions

We must also do this carefully. As we expose the dangers of being a lover of self, we must equally lift up the promise of being a lover of God. Emotions are a gift from God. Jesus wept, and Jesus rejoiced. He loved his Father, and he lamented to him. Jesus embodied our full humanity, feelings and all. Thus, the solution to the overemphasis on emotion is not to strip discipleship of feeling. We must make room for lament and celebration.

However, unlike Jesus we must recognize that our emotional life is tainted by the fall. Our emotions inevitably mislead us. Pastors have the honor of pointing the church to the God who does not mislead us, whose revelation clearly teaches what is good and true. Scripture unites us by giving us an agreed standard of goodness, compelling us to be good as we do good.

Shepherd the Weak and Uncertain

The cultural inertia of emotivism is so strong, and the self-love messaging so prevalent, that Christian leaders must work hard to equip Christians to think and live well in these difficult times. Preaching alone is inadequate. Exposing the folly of hyperindividualism, British documentarian Adam Curtis points to another way in which leaders must respond:[36]

In the age of the individual, it is wonderful to be free, to not be told by old, upper classes—the patricians—what to do, but on its downside you are on your own. That's fine when things go well, but when things go badly, you're weak and uncertain. We were going to be in this fantastic world, where we would be at the center of everything, and we would be in charge of our own lives, but it brings uncertainties with it.

When individualism bends under its own weight, the self is filled with weakness and uncertainty. We end up moving from source to source for meaning, swapping out identity after identity. As a result, individuals become despairing, confused, and lonely. It is here, in the rubble of misplaced trust, that we must respond with the reliability of God's grace and the certainty of his truth. Here are some practical ways we can shepherd the broken self.

Listen, Empathize, and Retell Stories

To minister to those who have been hurt and humbled by emotivism, I suggest three things which I can only address briefly here: 1) Listen to their story. 2) Empathize with their story. 3) Retell their story around Jesus.

Listen: As people navigate their own confusion and despair, they need a listening ear. Try to stay connected with people, within reason. Show up and ask questions like: What got you started down this path? What influences have been most formative for you? Why is this issue so important to you? You may discern a counseling opportunity or the presence of a surrogate authority.

Empathize: We must be willing to listen without passing immediate judgment. People who have deconstructed their faith will have done so with genuine doubts. People who have left the church often leave with heartfelt concerns.

We can sympathize with hurt, confusion, despair, and loneliness even if it is self-wrought. It is important to listen with a prayerful and compassionate heart. Ask the Holy Spirit to give you his compassion and kindness; he specializes in that.

Retell: As you listen, ask the Spirit for discernment. He has a way of cutting through the deceit to reveal what is true and untrue. The Spirit also helps us filter what we hear through the sieve of Scripture. Make a mental note of things that are repeated or untrue. Then ask the person if you can circle back to that topic or belief. It's important to affirm what is true before challenging what is untrue. This builds a bridge instead of burning one. For instance, "Yes, gender is something that Jesus cares deeply about. He elevated women in a time when they were marginalized by society." "It's obvious you've been hurt; I'm so sorry about that. The church can be a messy place."

When you challenge an untruth, try to do it in the form of a question. For instance, "Do you think it's possible politics has become more important to you than communion with Christ?" "When you said the leadership didn't care, did you have a conversation with each of the leaders?"

Then try to lead them to an aspect of Christ's character or ministry that corresponds with the lies they are believing. For instance, "I know you feel like everyone let you down, but have you considered that Christ, not the church, is your truest Advocate?" "It sounds like you feel guilty about how you have treated others; I want to remind you that Jesus is a Redeemer who delights to forgive your sin." "It sounds like this issue became the functional CEO of your life. Confess that and ask Jesus to replace its rule over your heart with his wise, gracious lordship." Ask the Spirit to bring about repentance and faith in Jesus and entrust the results to God.

Listen to their story, empathize with their story, and retell their story around Jesus. This may happen in one conversation or over the course of several conversations. Of course, these are the kinds of conversations we should never stop having.

LOVERS OF GOD

The ultimate solution to self-love is *philotheos*—God-love (3:4). A God-lover redirects their affections away from themselves back to the Lord. This begins with confession and matures into repentance as we face our gracious Savior. Though we fail him, he does not give us a one-star review. Instead, he forgives us and calls us to grow into our five-star standing with him. He does not see us as an obstacle to his purposes but as an object of his deep and glorious grace.

Loving God is better than loving ourselves because when we find something to love that is deeper and higher than ourselves, it not only satisfies us but frees us to serve others. In Jesus we discover a love which loves us back so deeply and tremendously that it changes how we perceive people. Lovers of God inhabit this divine love, and as a result, minister in counter cultural grace.

For years I kept score in my marriage. I silently noted what chores I had done and what chores my wife had not done. I was deeply aware of how emotionally available I was to her, and how emotionally unavailable she was to me. I thought of myself as a spiritual leader, clearly more faithful in devotional habits. I wanted to please her, but I also wanted her to measure up. The score-keeping would build up over time, and then I would erupt in self-righteous anger, screaming, "I just want you to meet me in the middle!"

This is not the way Jesus loves. He does not pledge his love for a 50 percent return on his investment. He gives everything—100 percent of his love and life, and then tells husbands, "Husbands, love your wives, as Christ loved the church and gave himself up for her" (Ephesians 5:25). How did Christ love the church? *By giving all of himself, not just part of himself.* Jesus did not angrily insist that we meet him in the middle. He went the distance for people who don't measure up in order to bring us home.

When we absorb how thoroughly loved we are by Jesus, we are freed to love those who don't love us back. As I learned to absorb and express God's love for me, my relationship with my wife changed. I was freed to serve her without calculation—to be vulnerable without demanding something in return. As a result, she has drawn closer to me. This has opened a door into a more intimate understanding of my wife, and as a result, I have come to appreciate and settle into her persistent, patient affection.

I have also learned more about God's love by inhabiting Robie's love. Her love has become a portal into divine love, allowing me to relax and be my true self in Christ— less of a record-keeper and more of a God-lover. This is what God's love is meant to do. It frees us from keeping score with him and one another, allowing us to relax and love him and others better. Divine love is a mark of the redemptive-historical age—the love of God poured out into our hearts through the Holy Spirit (Romans 5:5). It's no wonder Jesus said that this shared, otherworldly love would cause people to recognize us as *his* disciples. God's love flowing through God's people is a glowing neon sign in an anxious age.

PASTORING IN THE LAST DAYS

What time is it? Last and difficult days, marked by anxiety and love of self. Many want their ears tickled, and as a result, turn away from listening to the truth (2 Timothy 4:3-4). But we also live in the age of the Spirit, who is eager to work through leaders to spread the gospel and shepherd God's people into an ever-deepening knowledge of the Christ. He is intent on transforming lovers of self into lovers of God.

My grandfather, George Dodson, was a Baptist minister for over 60 years. In 2020, Robie and I had the privilege of visiting him in a hospice, where he lay dying of cancer. He ministered to many from his bed, reconciling people, comforting sufferers and assuring the weak. As he lay there, gaunt-faced and frail, my wife asked him, "Do you have any counsel for us in ministry before you go?" He replied, "There will always be truth-seekers and truth-tellers, and when the truth-tellers meet the truth-seekers, magic happens. Keep telling the truth."

Keep telling the truth.

When we do, gospel magic happens. People are translated out of the kingdom of darkness and into the kingdom of the beloved Son, transformed from one degree of glory to the next. We don't have to nail cultural exegesis, because Jesus was nailed to a cross. We don't have to talk people out of self-love, because the Spirit makes us lovers of God. When we tell the truth, God breaks the spell of deceit and gospel blessings are poured out.

THE UNWAVERING PASTOR

An unwavering pastor:

- tells the theological and cultural time.

- engages with personal anxiety by scrolling through God's graces.

- exposes the folly of self-love while demonstrating the blessedness of God-love.

- presents a biblical view of emotions.

- listens, empathizes, and retells individual stories around Jesus.

- keeps telling the truth so gospel magic can happen.

~~~6~~~

PREACH THE WORD

"Preach the word" (2 Timothy 4:2). Three words that summon up everything from aspirational zeal to serious self-doubt. Any given week, most of us plod from one extreme to the other. We labor over the word, thrilled by exegetical insights and word studies, but when it comes to assembling our nuts and bolts into a full-blown working sermon, self-doubt creeps in. "Have I been true to the text?" "Does my application land in the hearts of my people?" "Have I anticipated cultural objections?" So, how do we faithfully preach the word in chaotic times?

HEARING THE WORD

The answer to this question is not so much in preaching the word but in letting the word be preached to us. When we yield to the hammering effect of the word that we experience in sermon preparation, we welcome weakness and inadequacy. But when we take up the hammer, and refuse to put it down, we remain on the outside of God's word. The movement from hammering to being hammered, from above the text to under the text, is one of prayer.

In prayer, we respond to God's word and recognize it as his speech. We relate to him as a holy Speaker. His words solicit desperate pleas ("Help me, Lord!"), sincere repentance ("I have been controlling and self-centered this week, forgive me"), exuberant joy ("Glory to God!") or blessed insufficiency. When I hit a homiletic impasse, I often push myself away from the desk and go for a walk: "Spirit, what am I missing? What do you want me to hear? What do our people need? Speak to me, Lord." Our churches need not merely a well-prepared sermon but a well-worn preacher—a preacher who has been broken and cracked open so the golden words of God trickle in and transform them.

This confrontation between our inadequacy and God's infinite sufficiency is a diorama of pastoral ministry. We are called to something we cannot accomplish. We announce transformative news while remaining powerless to transform anyone. This is a good problem. If we had the power to change others, we would inevitably neglect those who offend or hurt us. We would transform people unevenly, missing areas that only an omniscient God can see. We would, no doubt, alter things that do not need altering, like personalities that rub us the wrong way. We would wish change immediately instead of gradually, causing Christians to forgo arduous yet rewarding sanctification that stretches over a lifetime. We would not preach the word but our insight, our stories, our knowledge, even our compassion—but not Christ.

But to preach the word is to preach Christ: not merely words about Christ but the person of Jesus himself. We proclaim a Christ who came not as a disembodied set of ideas but as the Word made flesh. Missiologist Andrew Walls draws our attention to the specificity of the incarnation:

"he became a person in a particular locality and in a particular ethnic group, at a particular place and time ... he became a historically and culturally conditioned man."[37] Likewise, when we preach, we communicate the eternal, unchanging word in a temporal, changing cultural form and idiom.

PREACHING THE WORD

Paul's famous imperative in 2 Timothy 4:2 is issued in the context of a conflict of authority, not the confines of a seminary classroom. It is situated between a divine charge and mythmaking. Some of Timothy's congregants are settling for getting their ears tickled: a phrase that means to look for interesting and juicy bits of information. This disposition inclines them to privilege other teachers over local elders and to follow myths instead of Scripture.

In an information age, this disposition is ubiquitous. Objections to our preaching often come from a podcast or YouTube video consumed by our congregants. While outside teachers can enrich their hearers, ear-tickling information lures people away into elitist knowledge untethered to the word of God. "Preach the word" is an urgent exhortation in subversive times.

Paul issues the order to preach the word from the divine court, the very "presence of God and of Christ Jesus" (v 1), who together possess the authority to judge the world. Preaching the word is a divinely authorized act from the one with authority over the living and the dead. Therefore, we should preach with a sense of heavenly accountability, discharging our responsibility with gravity.

But preaching isn't to be so heavenly minded that it is no earthly good. Preaching should not be done at a ninety-degree angle, shooting off into the theological atmosphere without touching down on earth. John Stott famously implores the preacher to proclaim God's word in 180 degrees.[38] Begin in the biblical world, most certainly, but direct your preaching to the present world. Be acquainted with the real struggles of the people you lead and the cultural myths they are tempted to believe.

The minister of the word stands between these two worlds. Straddling them is no easy task. For some, it is tempting to stay in the biblical world, throwing in an occasional application or cultural flourish. For others, cultural exegesis or life application is more alluring than mining the texts of Scripture. All are important, but there is no perfect blend in preaching. Instead, we should practice *congregational listening* to discern how best to engage with cultural myths.

Congregational listening is attending to *your* congregation. It is sitting down with souls and asking them what they struggle with, not generating imaginary application lists. We have to see their ears to preach to their hearts. A pastor who practices congregational listening pays attention to the issues that keep surfacing in the coffee shop or counseling office. They listen closely to the questions asked in small groups and discipleship relationships. They make a note of the objections frequently raised in theology and Bible classes. What patterns are you seeing in your people? What particular philosophies lead *them* astray? Listening to your congregation will enable you to discern which issues to address and how often to address them.

So, be relieved of striking a perfect balance between two worlds when preaching. Instead, listen to your church and the Spirit, and preach the word.

SUBVERSIVE AUTHORITIES

The greatest challenge to a ministry of the word is a competing authority. It is also the oldest challenge. When a usurping authority seeks to overturn Scripture, it typically subverts and replaces God's authority. In the Garden of Eden, Satan *subverted* God's authority by clandestinely setting himself up as a better authority: "Did God actually say, 'You shall not eat of any tree in the garden'?" (Genesis 3:1). While there is a place for questioning Scripture—we cannot learn if we do not inquire—Satan questioned God by suggesting that God was holding out on Adam and Eve (prohibiting *all* the trees). While Eve denies this, the bait is taken and the seed of doubt sown. She adds to God's command: "Neither shall you touch it, lest you die." While God said nothing about not touching the tree, he did say death would follow disobedience.

Next Satan *replaces* God's authority with his own authority: "You will not surely die. For God knows that when you eat of it your eyes will be opened, and you will be like God, knowing good and evil" (v 4–5). His subversion dangles like a worm right in front of them, his prey focused on what they do not have: *We do not know good and evil.* They clamp down, and with the subversive hook set, Satan yanks the line in a direct challenge to God's words. Maddeningly, he does all of this under the guise of beneficence: *Don't you want to be like God?* The devil challenges God's authority with the promise of reward, while dealing death. Similarly, contemporary competing authorities appear wholesome and just while seeking to subvert and replace God's word.

This ancient deception is a good reminder that preaching is spiritual war against a sinister opponent. We are not merely discussing theological ideas or dispensing life-enhancing advice. We are snatching souls from the fire. Therefore, we must not only preach the word but also pray the word. I often tell young preachers, "Once your sermon is done, it's time to pray the word into the people." After all, transformation is God's work, and it is better left in his hands.

What kinds of usurping authorities do you need to be on the lookout for? There are at least three types of subversive authority: philosophical, cultural, and personal.

Philosophical Authority

Thomas Aquinas famously quipped that philosophy is the handmaiden of theology. The medieval theologian effectively used Aristotelian philosophy to clarify and organize many theological topics, to shed more light on God himself. Similarly, Dr. John Frame uses perspectivalism to clarify the nature of God and his revelation.[39] However, philosophy is also used, not as a handmaiden of but as master over theology. The apostle Paul expresses concern about this when he says, "See to it that no one takes you captive by philosophy and empty deceit, according to human tradition, according to the elemental spirits of the world, and not according to Christ" (Colossians 2:8).[40] In Greek "see to it" is a single-word imperative meaning "to pay close attention to." *See to it, pastor!* Few else will.

Love of wisdom can kidnap the heart and carry us away from Christ. Accumulating knowledge can make us feel like experts, and if we aren't careful, the feeling of expertise will feed our pride. This is true for both the preacher and the church member: "Their theology is so out of whack!" "Our pastor is so out of step with the times." Expert knowledge can become a perch from which we judge others and others judge us.

Newfound expertise can even lead people to "turn away from listening to the truth and wander off into myths" (2 Timothy 4:4). When I drive around my city, I often see places that remind me of people who have wandered away from the faith: the womanizer, the lesbian, the skeptic, the materialist, the egomaniac. These heartbreaking memories move me to pray for their return, as in the parable of the prodigal son. But they also remind me to *see to it* that existing church members don't fall into a similar fate.

So, while philosophy may uncover truth and elucidate Scripture, it is not divine revelation. It does not lead us to Christ. When we permit any philosophy to rival and replace the word of God, we fall for the ancient ploy of the serpent. We must privilege the word over all other words, for it alone is "God-breathed" (2 Timothy 3:16, NIV).

Cultural Engagement

It seems that a new authority appears every week! How should we engage with competing philosophies? In Athens at Mars Hill, Paul employed an Affirm/Redeem/Confront (ARC) approach to Greek philosophy (Acts 17:22-34). He *affirmed* true insights from Greek philosophers and poets such as Epimenides and Aratus (v 28), building common ground with those other philosophies before exposing their shortcomings (v 29-30). He also *redeemed* their views by showing how God or the gospel is better than the presenting view. For instance, he redeems their passion for gods-in-temples by declaring Yahweh as the Creator who does not dwell in temples but who made everyone and everything (v 24-25). He also *confronted* those aspects of culture and philosophy that oppose biblical revelation. After affirming and redeeming the beliefs of the Greek philosophers, he confronts their idol-making and "wisdom" by assuring them that the true God will judge the world in righteousness, and then he calls them to repentance (v 30-31). With this framework in mind, let's examine two current competing authorities—one politically right-wing and another liberally left.

Two modern "philosophies" that exhibit both positive and negative traits, but also function as a competing authority to Scripture, are the QAnon conspiracy theory and Critical Race Theory. QAnon rapidly gained popularity for numerous reasons, one of which was its claim to have access to US security knowledge known as "Q clearance." This secret knowledge baited people into an elitist online group boasting special power to achieve right-wing political goals. Critical Race Theory (CRT) emerged out of Critical Theory, a sociological theory that originated with the Frankfurt School in the 1930s. It aimed to critique and change society based on some idea of what society should be, particularly through the use of power.

While the merits of each theory are hotly debated, they share something in common—a fascination with power. QAnon aims to achieve its ends with political power, CRT with racial power. Both groups of adherents desire to give power to what they perceive to be an underrepresented group. Whether we agree or disagree with a person or group, we should *affirm* their desire for representation and grant them the dignity to hold whatever they believe to be true. However, when these power-centric theories seek to solve social problems with the use of social, racial, and political power, the ends often do not justify the means. The QAnon-influenced insurrection at the US Capitol and a public-education overhaul based on social justice are such exclusivist misuses of power.[41]

So, while Critical Race Theory justly calls attention to imbalances of power in social relationships, it, like QAnon, requires all-or-nothing adherence. QAnon members proclaim you are "with us" or "against us," while CRT advocates put people in one of two categories: racist or anti-racist. There is no grace for in-between or alternative categories. Both theories insist that we must see everything through their lens; otherwise, we see and live incorrectly. Because totalizing theories call for total commitment, they erect an authority that competes with the word of God, which is something we must *confront*.

Scripture also calls for total commitment: "*All* Scripture is breathed out by God and profitable for teaching, for reproof, for correction, and for training in righteousness, that the man of God may be *complete*, equipped for *every* good work (2 Timothy 3:16–17, emphasis added). However, its totalizing claim is not made as a theory but as divine revelation. Furthermore, its central focus, Jesus, asserts that he is *the* way, *the* truth, and *the* life (John 14:6), and he calls Christians to follow *him*. Therefore, Jesus prohibits his followers from aligning *entirely* with another philosophy or theory which challenges his authority. While other theories may make positive contributions to our view of the world, these insights must be tested by Scripture and submitted to the lordship of Christ. When we challenge these powers, we will face resistance.

A small group of people in our church began listening to right-wing ear-tickling. When we asked them to comply with our landlord's mask policy during the COVID pandemic, one person compared the request to wearing amulets to ward off evil spirits and left the church. Another family, who had been with us for ten years, whose father I had mentored, and whose children I had dedicated, simply vanished. I was the brunt of no small criticism. When we confront the powers, the powers push back—a reminder that when Jesus called us, he called us to come and die.

Jesus turns power-centric theories on their head by using his power to suffer for those who oppress him (Philippians 2:5-8). He *redeems* broken grasps for representation by representing sinners as their substitute sacrifice for sin before the holy and just God (Hebrews 10:12). He grants *us* a voice with the Creator, when we deserved no voice at all (1 John 5:14). Jesus uses his authority to die in the place of the depraved and to shame the powers behind deceitful philosophies (Colossians 2:15). Jesus, unlike power-centric theories, is worthy of our submission. His use of power defies the categories of the left and the right, and it is this Christ we get to preach! So, when you preach the word, do so knowing that the gospel "is the power of God for salvation to all who believe" (Romans 1:16).

Of course, not all philosophical issues that threaten our churches and organizations have to be addressed "from the front." We should discern what is most effective in our own context, shepherding the flock through sermons, classes, newsletters, blogs, and social media. Some issues deserve a head-on approach; others require more of a slow drip, using forms of communication other than the pulpit.

While every Sunday is a power encounter, there are a variety of ways to wield the power of God's word: pastoral plea, wise counsel, bold exhortation, gentle correction, stiff rebuke, careful instruction, and patient teaching. Congregational listening will help us decide how to preach the power of God. Whatever comes, may we be found faithfully preaching the word when Jesus returns, in season and out of season; reproving, rebuking, and exhorting, with complete patience and teaching (2 Timothy 4:2).

Cultural Authority

Philosophies hammered out in the halls of the academy often trickle down into our culture. As certain viewpoints become embedded in the cultural psyche, it can be very difficult to resist them and embrace our status as a cognitive minority. The cultural and social pull to adopt these viewpoints is so strong, and the social penalties of ignoring them so high, that Christians often unreflectively comply. We swallow the blue pill.[42]

Paul gets at this when he says, "For the time is coming when people will not endure sound teaching" (v 3). His use of the word "*endure*" is tongue-in-cheek. These Christians aren't willing *to endure the hard work* required to grasp sound biblical teaching. Instead of using their heads, they want their ears tickled. As a result, they cave in to prevailing notions, welcoming popular influences while ignoring unpopular biblical views. They become biblically dishonest and culturally affirming.

Biblical dishonesty often emerges around issues promoted by cultural authorities. For instance, when the LBGTQ+ movement gained significant cultural ground, businesses began to integrate the rainbow flag into their logos and marketing materials. Once the gay agenda became mainstream, many Christians also began to fly the rainbow flag on their social-media accounts. Because mainstream culture shifted to affirming, Christians began to rethink or renounce historically orthodox views of biblical sexuality. Many became outspoken on the issue without doing serious biblical study. Some even canceled other Christians for not affirming the new view. However, many of these same Christians did not become outspoken against the oppression and murder of the unborn. Like corporations, they spoke up only when the broader liberal culture offered them social rewards. No such reward is offered by liberal media to those who are pro-life. This kind of Christianity allows mainstream liberal culture to act as a spiritual authority to set the moral agendas of our lives. But pastors must take their stand, lift up the lantern of God's word, and cast true moral and spiritual light into the world.

The left is not the only cultural force to function with anti-biblical authority. During the COVID pandemic, many right-wing media outlets excoriated Christians for wearing masks to protect themselves and others from contracting the coronavirus. Government mask mandates were cast as an infringement on religious liberty. Extremists called upon Christians to leave their churches if their leaders required them to wear masks. They did not encourage Christians to act like church family or process their concerns with local elders, but to jettison their brothers and sisters in favor of personal religious freedom. Right-wing, culturally-informed individual liberty was elevated over local qualified pastors who genuinely care for their flock, thoughtful biblical study and reflection, and the unity of the saints. Instead, rightist groups exalted spiritual independence and disregard of God-ordained authorities.

Both groups cancel Christians who refuse to replace the gospel with right or left ideologies. But Jesus calls Christians into a different way of living: to take up our cross and follow him daily, renouncing cultural authorities and pet ideologies in order to submit to his cruciform leadership. This isn't easy. Many of those who left our churches were friends, and all of them spiritual family. When a couple divorces, everyone in the family hurts. While these departures are often not meant to be a personal attack, the loss of friendship, distrust of our leadership, and drift from sound doctrine are heartbreaking. Leaders must create space for the Spirit to put our heart back together, to mend us in the silence and grief over lost family members and friends.

The church needs leaders who are biblically honest and courageous enough to teach sound doctrine. It is no mistake that the Greek word for "sound" means healthy. For the church to recover its strength, it will need consistent doses of healthy doctrine. But healthy doctrine, alone, is not enough. This instruction must be paired with rebuke and correction. When Titus faced similar circumstances in Crete, where entire families were led astray by competing authorities, Paul instructed him to "rebuke them sharply, that they may be sound in the faith" (Titus 1:13). Correction cleans the wound so that doses of healthy doctrine can treat it, making the church vibrant in faith.

Personal Authority

Philosophical authority trickles down from the academy into the broader culture and then to the individual. Philosophical views are embedded in cultural artifacts (corporations, products, memes), which are ingested by the masses through commerce and social media. In our historical moment, power-centric theories have influenced our culture creating a radically polarized society marked by right- and left-wing ideology.

Many of those we lead are radicalized (consciously and unconsciously) by the values of groups who promote these theories. When mainstream issues are controversial or grave, Christians often respond quickly out of a sensitive religious conscience, or to maintain or gain acceptance from either the right or the left. Absorbing and propagating views becomes an exercise in personal passion.

Paul writes, "... but having itching ears they will accumulate for themselves teachers to suit their own passions" (4:3). Today, these passions are fueled by the accumulation of ideological teachers through books, online articles, and social-media influencers. Much of this happens to the individual in isolation from community and good spiritual leadership. As a result, views are taken up without the wisdom of the community, careful theological reflection, or input from spiritual leaders who care. Meanwhile, passions fuel a sense of personal authority and ownership over a given issue. It is into this constellation of influences that we are called to preach the word.

The Greek word for passions, *epithymia*, combines the word for "desire" with a prefix that means "over" and is literally translated *over-desire*. When over-desire is directed toward Christ, it is just the right amount, but when passions are directed to anything else, the object of our desire overtakes us. In an age of information overload we can feel that we have to have all the answers. So, to offload anxiety and dissolve online pressure, we gather up information to help ourselves hone our expertise. But information alone simply makes us educated, not virtuous. Education plus the passions lead to angry, self-righteous tribalism, on the right and the left. This results in a sense of personal authority that trumps all other authorities, leading to division within the church.

But there is a better way and a better authority. Instead of privileging biased media headlines, overnight expertise, and quick online responses, we must seek the tutelage of Christ. We don't need teachers who suit our feelings, but we do need affection for the one true Teacher. It is only in the Lord that our passions are truly satisfied. We should encourage our churches to direct their desires toward the caring Father, the justifying Redeemer, and the Spirit of peace.

- **Caring Father:** Our personal, affectionate Father urges us to cast our cares upon him instead of

inert expertise, which cares nothing about us
(1 Peter 5:7).

- **Justifying Redeemer:** We are invited to trust the justifying Redeemer, who offers us his pristine righteousness in place of the blemished self-righteousness of expert knowledge (2 Corinthians 5:21).

- **Spirit of Peace:** We are offered the Comforter's genuine peace in place of angry outrage (John 14:26-27).

The Father, Son, and Holy Spirit work together to extend endless hope in what often feels like hopeless times. But for others to enjoy that hope, we must preach the word as *the* authority. We must admonish those in our care to trust divine counsel over the lure of so-called expert knowledge. We must implore them to cherish Christ's teachings over the many teachers that bargain for their beliefs. Preaching the word, in a world of competing authorities, is like broadcasting the location for refuge in a post-apocalyptic world. We must get the message out, but God alone can get them in.

PREACHING FOR THE REWARD
Is it all worth it? Slogging against subversive authorities, the pain of personal sanctification, and the onslaught of our anxious age? Absolutely! As Paul reflects on a life poured out in service to the gospel, he reveals the reward that kept him going—the crown of righteousness. He writes, "Henceforth there is laid up for me the crown of righteousness, which the Lord, the righteous judge, will

award to me on that day, and not only to me but also to all who have loved his appearing" (2 Timothy 4:8).

A crown is the rightful belonging of a monarch. It symbolizes his or her kingdom. This crown is made of righteousness, forged from the crown of the King of kings, and Paul says it belongs on our heads! This language is intended to conjure the moment when we will be ceremoniously crowned with the righteousness of Christ. On that day, justification by faith will become perfectly-felt justification. What we have struggled to believe, preach, and live out will be experienced in full as we are crowned—in fact, clothed from head to toe—with righteousness. We will never again second guess our motives, doubt God's promises, or strain to be holy.

This righteousness is not only for us; it is for all who have loved his appearing (v 8). Those we have led will kneel beside us to receive the same golden crown upon their heads. Leaders will witness their followers' crowning ceremony. They too will shine like stars. It is no wonder Paul refers to those he discipled as his "glory and joy" (2 Thessalonians 4:16). Leadership affords us this wonderful reward—crowns compounded—as we gaze into the glory of Christ.

Run the race, fight the good fight, and keep the faith. If you do, when you stand before the Lord of glory and his righteousness kisses your head, inundates your body, and animates your soul, you will think to yourself, "It was all worth it. The hurt, the sorrow, the loss, the pain. Everything. Every single bit. *You* are worth it, Lord." Let's keep our eyes on the crown.

THE UNWAVERING PASTOR

An unwavering pastor:

- yields to the word while also preaching the word.

- practices congregational listening to discern which cultural myths to engage with.

- recognizes the value of philosophy while refusing to concede the ultimate authority of Scripture.

- engages with culture using a paradigm of Affirm, Redeem, Confront (ARC).

- challenges individual authority with the sacrificial authority of Christ and his word

- orients desires toward the satisfying presence of the Father, Son, and Spirit.

- perseveres to lay hold of the crown of righteousness.

～～ 7 ～～

CONTINUE IN THE FAITH

It was the second Tuesday of the month; a half-day retreat was required for all staff members. I contemplated sticking around the house, but the Spirit nudged me toward the Lady Bird Wildflower Center, an arboretum with sprawling trails across Texas land. After walking for half a mile, I sat down and opened the Bible. The words struck like a Spirit-anointed sermon: "As for you, always be sober-minded, endure suffering, do the work of an evangelist, fulfill your ministry" (2 Timothy 4:5). I was preoccupied with what *others* were doing to me, but the Spirit said, *As for you, here is your calling: be sober-minded, endure suffering, do the work of an evangelist, and fulfill your calling.* When we are overwhelmed or discouraged, it's helpful to come back to the simplicity of our call.

SOBER-MINDED

A sober-minded person possesses mental and spiritual clarity that arises from honest communion with God. Because God is the most clear-minded thinker ever to exist, he sees the world, our lives, and our ministry with 20/20 vision. His thoughts about us and our ministry are always true. His take is never tainted by impure motives. He never makes a wrong decision because he wants to please people. He always makes right decisions because he seeks the highest good—his eternal glory. This enables him to chart a clear, righteous path for his people. Pastors who stay close to *this* God are sober-minded.

An overwhelmed student came to Professor of Spiritual Theology and veteran pastor Eugene Peterson for advice. She felt distant from God, so she read more and more Scripture, but felt further and further away from him. Eugene told her to read less Bible, and handed her Dostoyevsky. When we're struggling we need less volume and more depth. We need authors who articulate our struggles in ways that help us feel understood. That's why Lamentations, the Psalms of Lament, exist and why one of Jesus' titles is the Man of Sorrows—not merely to inform us but to validate our sorrows.

At the end of 2021, I was walking toward our church building and felt something inside me break, like a rubber band stretched too far. Snap! In an instant I was emotionally decoupled from the church. I had no reserves. As I stumbled in grief, God ministered to me through Lamentations: "He has made my flesh and my skin waste away; he has broken my bones; he has besieged and enveloped me with bitterness and tribulation" (Lamentations 3:4-5). A sovereign breaking. A deep revealing of my utter weakness. A severe mercy that would drive me deep into the presence of God.

The grief gave way to waiting: "The LORD is good to those who wait for him ... It is good that one should wait quietly for the salvation of the LORD" (3:25-26). The two things repeated here are "waiting" and "good." We live in a society that thinks faster is better. We prize the efficient pastor, not the contemplative pastor. But God *does good* to those who *wait* for him. In the waiting, we recover depth.

It is easier to wait in the quiet: noiseless streets, a quiet study, remote trails. In the quiet God saves us. He rescues us from grief, from sin, from busyness, from being a pastor, to love us like a son or a daughter. Although the term "quiet time" has fallen on hard times, it is perhaps more needed than ever. Quiet pastors are sober-minded pastors.

Any number of things can keep us from waiting. It's possible to be so entrenched in our *sufferings* that we don't think clearly about people and circumstances. A spike in complaints to our spouse or close friends can be a sign that our thinking is slipping. There's a place for processing disappointment with trustworthy people, but when the complaints pile up, it can be hard to see over them.

Coping mechanisms also dull spiritual alacrity. Eugene Peterson had his bouts with the bottle. In his journals, he confesses that evening whiskey impeded his morning prayers. This led to stretches of abstention.[43] When I'm tempted to cope without Christ, I reach for movies. They are an escape from the weight of responsibility and the heartache of ministry, but when the credits roll no actor is left to comfort me. Only the Director of all things brings true comfort. Intoxication with anything other than the triune God dulls our senses and impedes our judgment.

How do we cultivate sober-mindedness in the midst of suffering? When a cyclist drafts behind another cyclist, they position themselves inches behind the rider. This keeps them in their slipstream, reducing headwind and increasing speed by up to five miles an hour. But when a cyclist falls out of the draft, they have to expend two or three times the energy to get back into position. The rider has to "burn a match" to return, consuming a lot of energy.

When we stay close to God, we draft on his truth and grace. His presence carries us through everyday responsibilities and difficult times. But when we fall out of communion with God, we begin to rely on our own effort. Everything becomes harder, every blow heavier. We are quickly depleted and easily overwhelmed. Strategy, intellect, personality, and giftings wear out.

Fortunately, we don't have to burn a match to get back into God's renewing presence. We just confess our need, receive his comfort, and trust in his promises. We draft grace. Staying close to God makes our mind clearer and our heart brighter, freeing us to lead well. Stay close to God and he will keep you sober-minded.

Clear the Clutter

Even if we think well, our minds are easily cluttered with other important things: sufferers, church health, vision, family, personal holiness, and pain. Unless we have a habit of taking these things to the Lord in prayer, our heart and mind will become so crowded that we will be unable to think straight. Leaders that last develop a regular pattern of taking the clutter to God.

I find it helpful to pray through my specific roles each morning: father, husband, pastor, author and preacher. I begin with the Lord's Prayer: "Our Father in heaven, hallowed be your name. Help me to hallow you as a tender father, a loving husband, a wise pastor, a creative, skilled, truth-telling author, and an anointed preacher." Along the way I sometimes linger on a role: "Lord, I've been snapping at my kids. Forgive me. Give me your heart of mercy for them and help me not to pounce on every error."

However, after several years of praying in this way, my requests began to feel like burdens. I felt that I was primarily drawing attention to my role failures. Then it occurred to me that I was beginning each day with my roles and not my identity. Jesus taught us to pray, "Our Father," not *Our Employer*. He didn't hire us just to execute various roles; he redeemed us to live as his very own children. When I realized that my prayer was off kilter, I began praying like a son. It changed my prayers and my heart. Now I begin by saying something like, "Lord, thank you that I get to be your son today. That I begin the day with your favor and love. Help me to stay there, to live out of this blessed grace."

Praying as the child of a caring Father changes the way we speak to God about things that crowd our heart. When I pray to God for sufferers, it is especially helpful: "Lord, I am inadequate for the porn-addicted husband, the skeptical student, the critical church member. You are more than adequate. I give them to you. You love them so much more than I do. Only you can change and heal Lord, so please do it."

Prayer has a way of shifting the weight of pastoral care and ministry responsibility off our shoulders and onto God's. The important clutter begins to take its rightful place in the presence of our immense God. Slowly, we move into a settled sense of who we are in Christ, freeing us to pray with hope and relief. But when we're far from God, responsibilities crowd him out, and we are quickly overwhelmed.

Prayer clears the fog like nothing else. When we relate to God from our adoptive place in his family, we emerge refreshed and focused on what he has called us to do. Led by a great and caring God, we are freed to lead others well. When he is up close, other cares line up behind his tremendous presence.

ENDURE SUFFERING

On some days these gospel truths pump through my bloodstream like supercells, giving me energy for ministry. On other days I move in slow motion. In a season when gospel truths weren't flowing through my system, and arrows peppered me every week, I thought, "Why continue? I could get a job where there is less pain. I have other gifts. Why not look around?" These are natural thoughts in suffering, and how we handle them is significant.

Endure suffering (2 Timothy 4:5; also translated "endure evil") isn't an aspect of our job description we get excited about. It's one we tend to forget. As I watched the tears trickle down the face of a pensive, middle-aged father, I was moved by what death does. Ministry brings the reality of a hurting world home. As we minister to the bereaved, we absorb a cost exacted by evil. A similar experience happens when we comfort the sick, counsel the skeptical, and correct the stumbling sinner. When we put people first, we often experience their pain secondhand. While not as acute as their experience, the hurt is real and fairly frequent in our calling.

But there is an even deeper pain we often carry—an aching hurt from the wounds others inflict upon us. Very often, people are unaware of how their criticism stings or their abandonment makes us ache. At other times, the attack is open and spite-filled. Name-calling and harsh words can penetrate deeply. Trapped inside, words can rattle around for years, bumping up against the walls of our heart over and over. This makes leadership particularly painful—a regular exposure to first- and secondhand pain.

We brush with first and secondhand evil not only because we live in a fallen world but also because we face a great enemy. Our calling comes with a villain attached. Satan and those under his power come to steal, kill, and destroy. That is *his* job description. His coming is not probable but certain, his attack personal.[44] The devil's aim is to lure Christians away, break the spirit of their leaders, and destroy all that is holy and good. This evil we must endure. Jesus came for opposite reasons: "I came that they might have life and have it abundantly" (John 10:10). Just as Satan is the antichrist, so Christ is the anti-Satan. Jesus didn't break into earth to steal; he came to recover and restore. Instead of seeking to kill, he surrendered his life so we can live. Jesus does not destroy but imparts resurrection life.

The difference between Satan and Christ is vividly depicted in pastoral terms. A crowded sheep pen attracts thieves and wolves who maraud for fresh meat. But there is always a way out. Christ says, "I am the door of the sheep" (v 7). Christ is our exit from Satan's cruelty. As shepherds, we implore the sheep to run to the exit, preaching Christ and corralling the flock toward the door. We coax, guide, yell, wave, and point souls to their only escape from Satan's schemes. We know there is no other way out.

But we aren't just shepherds; we are also sheep among wolves (Matthew 10:16). Satan doubles his efforts to disorient and discourage those who dedicate their lives to rescuing sheep. He draws on his armory of affliction to dissuade us from pointing people to Christ. This is perilous work, but Christ is our saving exit too. He is our door of escape, our exit into green pasture. Jesus is the great Shepherd who pastors struggling pastors.

When I went on my first sabbatical, I had a very clear question for God: "Do you want me to continue pastoring?" I was open to any answer but favored a "No." God's answer came during the Scripture readings at the monastery of the Society of St. John the Evangelist. The first text was John 21:15-17: *If you love me, feed my sheep.* As I responded to the reading, I knew this was the Lord's reply and reluctantly agreed. The next reading was from Ezekiel 34: "I myself will be the shepherd of my sheep, and I myself will make them lie down, declares the LORD GOD" (v 15). Yahweh declares that he will be the shepherd of his people, twice, with first-person pronouns: "I myself." The entire passage is stuffed with God's unequivocal resolution to do the shepherding. Although God had renewed my call to pastor his flock, he pledged himself to do the shepherding in the next breath!

Too often I pastor as though it's up to me to rescue the lost, shepherd the hurting, and make people lie down in God's presence. But God promises he will rescue, feed, and make his sheep lie down. Yahweh does the work. This came as an immense relief. God was asking me to do something that he himself would do. And so it is with you, pastor. He will shepherd your people. It's up to him to make busy people slow down and cherish God's presence, not us. Only he can move a sinner to repent or grow. He beckons us to be sheep before we are shepherds: to lie down in the lush pastures of his nourishing presence. *This is how we endure.*

Ministry Is War

Marty McGinn, a veteran church planter visited my evangelism class in seminary. He stood at the front of the class with a stack of white papers face down in front of him and began to tell stories. After each story, he reached down to pull up a sheet and held it up to us. The first page read "Church planting is warfare." After the second story, he held up another piece of paper that read, "Church planting is warfare." He told a third story and held up another page that said, "Church planting is warfare." He repeated this several more times. *Ministry* is warfare.

In war soldiers slog through harsh conditions, get the wind knocked out of them, and are wounded. Why do they endure it? To achieve victory over the enemy. We too fight, not to achieve but to claim victory. Jesus' triumph over sin, death, and Satan is for people, communities, churches, the world. Don't give up. His cause is the greatest on earth. Take heart—Jesus is coming back to claim his spoils.

Until then, corral his sheep toward the door of life. Guide his people through dirt and ash into soft, verdant pastures. And remember, Christ is their crystal spring, not your perfectly crafted sermon. Jesus is their fresh pasture, not your warm pastoral presence.[45] The Son of God is their Savior, not our strategies. Jesus, alone, imparts abundant life. So, look to Christ. Hope in Christ. Preach Christ. Rest in Christ. Jesus Christ is the only leader who will never let his people down. Be ok with that. Be thrilled with that. His power and grace are unrivaled. Endure with Christ. The war is worth it.

DO GOSPEL WORK

Paul also tells Timothy to do the work of an evangelist (2 Timothy 4:5), but Tim doesn't fit the modern profile of a soul-winner.[46] He's not slick or in it for money. He isn't eloquent or bold. Thousands don't gather to hear his sermons. Tim is a struggling pastor with a flock to shepherd, and yet Paul exhorts him to do the work of an evangelist.

Many pastors struggle with evangelism. They often prefer to teach or counsel, preach or disciple. But New Testament scholar Robert Yarbrough describes an evangelist as "a proclaimer of the gospel's good news."[47] That's work we can all do—gush about the goodness of the gospel. And it's imperative that we do that because faith comes by hearing the word of Christ (Romans 10:17). No one ever saw a person do a good work and conclude, "I must be a sinner deserving judgment before a holy God and desperately need redemption that only comes through faith in the death and resurrection of Jesus Christ." To reach that conclusion requires a message of words.[48]

Given the significant internal demands on Timothy's ministry, Paul likely wanted to draw his attention to evangelistic needs beyond his church. When leaders face significant conflict, needs in the community, or increased demand for counseling, they have to devote lots of energy to gospel ministry inside the church. But, if we're not attentive in those seasons, we may neglect gospel ministry outside the church.

Some leaders face an opposite temptation—neglecting pastoral care for the sake of the mission. They evangelize people and plant churches but fail to disciple and shepherd them. Pope Francis combines both missional and pastoral concerns by conceiving of the church as a field hospital.[49] While the church is always on mission in the battlefield, it also pitches hospital tents to care for the injured and lame. Pastoral care is part of the mission: patching up souls and sending them back out.

So when Paul tells Timothy to do the work of an evangelist, he is telling him to do gospel work. He doesn't expect Timothy to abandon his congregation for itinerant preaching. Rather, he expects him to be about the gospel. This includes getting the gospel out into the world *and* down into the church. Some people need to hear the good news for salvation and others need it for sanctification, but everybody needs the gospel.

FULFILL YOUR MINISTRY

Finally, Paul reminds us to fulfill our ministry (2 Timothy 4:5). The word "fulfill" means "to complete." When I contemplated leaving my church, I was enduring a sustained personal attack with very little support. The whole thing felt unbearable, so I called a mentor at 2:00 a.m. Struggling to wake up, he mumbled, "Jonathan?" I replied,

"Hi, Doug, I'm sorry it's so early but I need your help." He asked me to share what was going on. After listening, asking good questions, and empathizing, he said, "Jonathan, you can finish but never quit." But I wanted to quit! I knew God hadn't called me away, but pain was pushing me out the door.

How do we know whether we are finishing or quitting? We can start by heeding the adage "Never quit on a bad day" (or week or month!). We rarely make wise big decisions when we're hurting. A finisher also considers practical questions: If I leave, who will replace me? Is God calling me to something, or am I just avoiding responsibility? What do my peers and mentors think? Have they confirmed the call to finish? How is my family coping? But discerning the difference between finishing and quitting is more spiritual. It's a gut feeling—a sense of the Spirit's direction. Deep down I knew that if I left, I would leave things undone. I would be quitting. That might not be the case with you. God may be calling you to finish, but even if we do quit, God still loves quitters. Physically and spiritually exhausted, Elijah threw in the towel while sitting under a tree. But the Lord met him with angelic ministry and strengthened him to resume his ministry. There are times to finish a ministry and move on, but may we never quit following our faithful and tender Shepherd.

After being poured out like a drink offering, Paul knows he has completed the race (2 Timothy 4:6). Recalling personal harm and opposition to the gospel he reminded him, "the Lord stood by me and strengthened me, so that through me the message might be fully proclaimed and all the Gentiles might hear it" (v 17). When it feels like everyone has left, the Lord stands by you. When you are weak, he pledges to strengthen you. The Lord Jesus proudly stands by ministers to strengthen them for and with the gospel's good news. One day you will finish your current post, and you will eventually finish your race, at which point the Lord will rescue you from every evil deed and bring you safely into his heavenly kingdom (v 18). Evil does not have the last say; Christ does. Until then, may we remain sober-minded, endure suffering, do gospel work, and fulfill our ministry for the glory of God.

THE UNWAVERING PASTOR

An unwavering pastor:

- seeks to be sober-minded by staying close to God.

- clears the clutter through regular, dependent prayer.

- endures suffering by trusting Jesus to do the heavy shepherding.

- gets the gospel out into the world and down into the church.

- fulfills the ministry with confidence that the Lord stands by us.

〰 8 〰

GRACE TO ALL

As I write this final chapter from a snowy lake house in northern Minnesota, I am reminded of the warmth God's people can bring into our lives. This trip was unexpected. When I stepped away from the church for some impromptu leave, Eric Magnuson, a member in our church, texted me to offer his parents' lake house as a place to retreat to. The offer was touching and seemed impossible for a variety of reasons, but I felt that I should leave the text in my Messages app. Then, one Sunday I caught up with Eric at the sound booth. He said that he'd talked to his parents and that they wanted to pay for my airfare and rental car to make the trip a possibility.

I don't even know Eric's parents. Their offer awakened something easily forgotten in divisive times—the love of the church. As I prepare to return to Austin, I am not just going back to war; I am going home. I am returning to my spiritual family: brothers and sisters who love me. Although our churches may struggle to express their love for us at times and we fail to recognize it, there is a divine, scarlet bloodline that binds us together.

COME TO ME

Paul concludes his transparent letter by repeating a phrase: "Do your best to come to me soon" (2 Timothy 4:9, 21). There he goes, yearning again. Not *Come when you can* but *Get here soon*. Not *Make an effort to see me* but *Do your best*. Paul hasn't gone dark, boarded up his heart, or left the ministry. He still loves the church and longs to see his spiritual son.

Some family members are especially close. We click. We know they're safe—that we can rely on them for support—and we enjoy being with them. Spend time with these people! Indulge yourself! Contact that old friend, meet up with the life-giving church member, lean into that trusted leader. Prioritize life-giving relationships.

The Lord knows you have many demanding relationships. You need the church as much as the church needs you. So when you feel desperate, let people know. Paul seeks to expedite Timothy's arrival in verse 21: "Do your best to get here *before winter*." Tell your spiritual children when you need their warmth, even if it's before a frigid season.

RECONCILED PEOPLE

As pastors, we see damage in the church, but we also witness the restorative power of the family of God. Paul asks Timothy to bring Mark with him. You may recall that Paul and Mark had a sharp disagreement and parted company. Yet somewhere along the way, they were reawakened to the reconciling love of Jesus and embraced one another as brothers, like family. Once Paul had left in a huff, but now he's inviting Mark's presence.

In the midst of pain, it can be hard to imagine getting close again to those who hurt us. There were some people who were part of our church that I didn't really want to see again. But they were still family. I told myself that I would reconcile with them if they asked, but I would never be friends with them again. I felt it was ok to feel that way, and not wrong to refuse a friendship. But as the lingering pain recedes, and we recall the scarlet love of Christ, may we remain openhearted to the restorative power of the gospel in the family of God. Despite his fractured relationship with Mark, Paul shows us redemptive possibilities in Christ—more than friends, they resumed their partnership in the gospel!

Have you sworn off reconciliation with some of the people who hurt you? Peter incredulously asked Jesus if we should forgive those who hurt us up to seven times. Jesus answered, "Seventy times seven" (Matthew 18:22, CSB). The point isn't to keep track of how much we forgive but to forgive as we have been forgiven—endlessly. To be sure, forgiveness doesn't obligate friendship, but it does obligate hope—the hope that even estranged family members can become partners in the gospel once again. Wouldn't this be a wonderful testimony to the power of the cross? To embrace a returning church member who left and even hurt you. While we need not say, *Do your best to get to me soon*, Jesus spurs us to treat those who hurt us with his profound, forgiving love.

STILL ON MISSION
There are a lot of other people in the closing remarks in 2 Timothy 4. Luke, Paul's faithful companion, is with him.

Titus, Crescens, and Tychicus have been sent to other places. Others remain at their post. And locked away in prison, Paul remains on mission. Despite his painful experiences, he refuses to hang it up. Recalling Jesus' faithful presence, Paul declares that God strengthened him "so that through me the message might be fully proclaimed and all the Gentiles might hear it" (2 Timothy 4:17). Sensing the end is near, he reflects on the fulfillment of his calling to carry the name of Christ before the Gentiles and kings (v 18; Acts 9:15). How inspirational, when Paul would have been justified in finishing his ministry much earlier. Yet he pressed into his calling, reaching the nerve center of the Gentile world. May we remain true to our calling, whatever it is, so that God's gospel can flow through us. But there's something else compelling about Paul's mission.

God's message didn't come through Paul just in his words but also in his weakness. Incarcerated in the heart of the pagan Roman Empire, Paul's sorrowful abandonment became an opportunity to demonstrate the faithful presence of Jesus. His inability to serve others became an occasion for others to serve him. His chains became a foil for the unbound gospel. He stared down the lion's mouth and remained hopeful about God's deliverance. The unstoppable grace of God was proclaimed through Paul's limiting circumstances. When the world witnesses an inadequate man clinging to the infinitely adequate God, evangelism is enfleshed. When we are transparent about our frailty, people get to marvel at God's strength.

On the Sunday when I announced my pastoral leave, I told the congregation that I didn't have the emotional strength to preach. I shared that I was broken, zapped of emotional energy, and simply couldn't pastor them. But I also told them that I anticipated God's grace would shine through my cracks and assured them that I was not bitter or angry, only depleted. A young woman came up to me afterwards and said, "That is the best sermon you ever preached. I have never seen anything like this in a church." Tears formed in her eyes as she explained how God had confronted her unrealistic expectations of church and moved her to put her ultimate trust in Jesus. As a result, our church became her family. What she witnessed that day was the all-sufficient grace of God vividly flowing through a totally insufficient pastor. Even in our sufferings—perhaps especially in them—we can become a living illustration of God's grace poured out for sinners in Jesus. We become evidence of the possibilities of a life rooted in the love of Christ.

A few weeks before I returned to pastoring, we received a package in the mail. As my wife opened the box, I saw ceramic through the bubble wrap and laughed, "Another couple's gift for the kitchen." But as she peeled back the wrap, I saw a black kintsugi bowl with large gold veins running through it. What was once broken was now mended and beautified. A group of church members who loved me in my brokenness had sent me a symbol of God's gracious, tender work in me during this season.

Paul closes his letter with a flurry of family greetings and a personal note to Timothy: "The Lord be with your spirit" (2 Timothy 4:22). Wherever you are, may the Lord also be with your spirit: comforting, sustaining, healing, and thrilling you with all that he is for you in Jesus. May his presence extend and his grace overflow, just as Paul wishes it to when he concludes, "Grace be with you [plural]." Indeed, may God's precious, sustaining, and costly grace be with all our churches. Amen.

ACKNOWLEDGMENTS

This book wouldn't have been written without the tremendous support of City Life Church. You encouraged me with notes, Scriptures, coffee, prayers, and a beautiful kintsugi bowl. I am particularly indebted to our elders, who supported the broken, weak, weepy, and slow Jonathan. Thank you Peter, John, and Matt. You are such faithful shepherds.

Mom and Dad, you refreshed me with your attentive love and hospitality while I was in Colorado. It was just what I needed. Thank you, Magnusons, for your generosity.

Thanks, Don, for working hard to get this book to the right publisher, and Brian Thomasson, for your enthusiastic support and editorial help throughout.

My wife, Robie, deserves the most gratitude. Honey, you are behind every chapter, holding me up. You gave me space to weep through my sorrows and work toward hard-won joys, without a single frustrated word or condemning outburst. You are my greatest source of wisdom and encouragement. I love you.

Glory to our Lord, who pursues us with unstoppable grace.

ENDNOTES

1 All definitions of Greek words are taken from Walter Bauer and others, *A Greek-English Lexicon of the New Testament and Other Early Christian Literature*, 3rd ed. (University of Chicago Press, 2000).

2 I use a pseudonym in this story and most stories in this book.

3 Paul often uses "the faith" and "the gospel" interchangeably: "... if indeed you continue in the faith, stable and steadfast, not shifting from the hope of the gospel that you heard, which has been proclaimed in all creation under heaven, and of which I, Paul, became a minister" (Colossians 1:23). Here he exhorts Christians to persevere by trusting in the content of the gospel/the faith. However, sometimes he uses "the faith" to emphasize not the gospel we believe but our belief in the gospel: "Only let your manner of life be worthy of the gospel of Christ, so that whether I come and see you or am absent, I may hear of you that you are standing firm in one spirit, with one mind striving side by side for the faith of the gospel" (Philippians 1:27).

4 Eugene Peterson, *This Hallelujah Banquet: How the End of What We Were Reveals Who We Can Be* (Waterbrook Press, 2021), p 15-16.

5 Bryan Chapell, *1–2 Timothy and Titus* (Crossway, 1998), loc. 3024.

6 Charlie Warzel, "I Talked to the Cassandra of the Internet Age" *New York Times*, Feb. 4, 2021.

7 Michael Goldhaber, "Attention Shoppers!" *Wired*, December, 1997; https://www.wired.com/1997/12/es-attention/.

8 Barna Research Group, "38% of U.S. Pastors Have Thought About Quitting Full-Time Ministry in the Past Year" 2021; https://www.barna.com/research/pastors-well-being/ (accessed Mar. 9 2022)

9 Regarding the Pauline use of "not ... but," Fee notes Paul's pattern of contrasting something unfitting of the Holy Spirit with something that is. Fee writes, "Thus Paul's intent goes something like this: 'For when God gave us his Spirit, it was not timidity that we received, but power, love, and self-discipline.'" Gordon Fee, *1 & 2 Timothy, Titus* (Baker, 2017), p 227.

10 Thomas Watson, "How We May Read the Scriptures with Most Spiritual Profit" in *Puritan Sermons* (1674; reprint, Richard Owen Roberts, 1981), vol. 2, p 62.

11 Helpful resources on these topics, from brief to thorough, include: Rebecca McLaughlin, *The Secular Creed: Engaging Five Contemporary Claims* (The Gospel Coalition, 2021); Kathy Keller, *Jesus, Justice, and Gender Roles* (Zondervan, 2014); Thaddeus J. Williams, *Confronting Injustice without Compromising Truth* (Zondervan, 2021); Esau McCaulley, *Reading While Black* (IVP [US], 2020).

12 Christianity has been scrutinized through three national events: the Obergefell v Hodges Supreme Court case regarding gay marriage in 2015, the Women's March for gender equality in 2017, and the lightning-rod murder of George Floyd in 2020.

13 In chapter 5, I examine how feelings have distorted our understanding of goodness and how we should respond to this distortion.

14 There are three main ways to answer this question. We can answer it theologically, making a case from Scripture; sociologically, deconstructing broken cultural expressions of the faith, which are untrue to orthodox Christianity; and pastorally, embodying the goodness and love of Christ in our response. If we only offer theological and sociological responses, we fail to pastor the whole person.

15 This is a reference to a scene in *The Matrix Reloaded* (2003). In this famous scene, the main character, Neo, stops a hail of bullets coming toward him by holding out his hand in front of his body and suspends the bullets in mid-air.

16 Barry Corey, *Love Kindness: Discover the Power of a Forgotten Christian Virtue* (Tyndale Momentum, 2016), p xx.

17 Tim Shorey, "Assume You Are Wrong," The Gospel Coalition, January 21, 2021, https://www.thegospelcoalition.org/article/assume-you-are-wrong/ (accessed Feb. 17 2022).

18 @ElliotPage, Instagram, Dec 1, 2020.

19 I am using a pseudonym.

20 This bi-directional dwelling of Jesus—"you in me, and I in you"—is the result of the Spirit. Jesus explains to the disciples, "He dwells with you and will be in you" (John 14:17). So while the disciples are anxious about Jesus' departure, he comforts them with the promise of his presence through the Spirit, which is one reason why the Holy Spirit is called the Spirit of Jesus (Philippians 1:19). The Spirit is the relational glue of our newly constructed relationship with Jesus.

21 Dr. Greg Beale describes these three figures as the loyal soldier, lawful athlete, and laboring farmer in his helpful sermon on 2 Timothy 2: https://www.thegospelcoalition.org/sermon/2-timothy-2/ (accessed Feb. 17 2022).

22 C.S. Keener, *The IVP Bible Background Commentary: New Testament* (1 Corinthians 9:24–25); (InterVarsity Press, 1993).

23 This is a fictional person drawn from a variety of people I have encountered in ministry.

24 See the helpful, though sometimes dated book by John Stott, *Christ in Conflict: Lessons from Jesus and His Controversies* (IVP [US], 2013), p 19-20.

25 "Jesus juke" is a term coined by Christian author Jon Acuff in 2010. It usually describes when someone turns a light conversation into something serious and "holy" to demonstrate their spiritual superiority.

26 Gordon Fee, *1 & 2 Timothy, Titus* (Baker, 2012), p 251.

27 TARDIS stands for "Time And Relative Dimensions In Space" and refers to the time travel machine that British science fiction character Doctor Who travels in. The TARDIS has a cloaking technology that allows it to take the form of its natural surroundings. Unfortunately, this technology failed, and the TARDIS is stuck in the form of a British Police Box (callbox) from a trip to England.

28 American Psychiatric Association, "APA Public Opinion Poll – Annual Meeting 2020," September 14-16, 2020; https://www.psychiatry.org/newsroom/apa-public-opinion-poll-2020 (accessed Feb. 17 2022).

29 During the initial month of lockdown in March 2020, Pornhub reported a spike in viewing across 30 countries. After offering their premium service for free, India saw a 95 percent surge in porn use; https://www.complex.com/life/2020/03/pornhub-traffic-increases-amid-coronavirus-outbreak https://www.firstpost.com/tech/news-analysis/pornhub-sees-95-per-cent-spike-in-indian-viewership-during-coronavirus-lockdown-report-8234401.html (accessed Feb. 17 2022).

30 A federal emergency hotline for people in emotional distress registered a more than 1,000 percent increase in April 2020 compared with the same time the previous year; https://www.washingtonpost.com/news/powerpost/paloma/the-health-202/2020/05/04/the-health-202-texts-to-federal-government-mental-health-hotline-up-roughly-1-000-percent/5eaae16c60 2ff15fb0021568/?itid=ap_paigewinfield%20cunningham (accessed Feb. 17 2022).

31 Madeline Wells, "SF Bay Area restaurants are still struggling. Returning customers don't see that," SF Gate, January 23, 2021; https://www.sfgate.com/food/amp/SF-Bay-Area-restaurants-customers-rude-Yelp-review-16333535.php?__twitter_impression=true (accessed Feb. 17 2022).

32 Walk the Moon, "All I Want" on *What if Nothing,* November 2017.

33 Alasdair MacIntyre, *After Virtue: A Study in Moral Theory* (University of Notre Dame Press, 1994), p 12. Various words are used to refer to this self-centered ethic: the buffered self, emotivism, expressive individualism, hyperindividualism. In philosophy, Charles Taylor explains emotivism through the concept of the buffered self in Taylor, *A Secular Age* (Belknap Press, 2007). Emotivism is the term used in ethics to denote a feeling-based ethic. Sociologists describe this impulse as "expressive individualism." See Robert N. Bellah, *Habits of the Heart: Individualism and Commitment in American Life* (University of California Press, 1996), p 333-34. For a more accessible description of hyperindividualism's impact on society, see David Brooks, *The Road to Character* (Random House, 2015) and his follow-up, *The Second Mountain* (Random House, 2019).

34 Charles Taylor, *Sources of the Self* (Harvard Press, 1989), p 3.

35 I compare the Beatitudes of Christ with the functional secular "beatitudes" of our times, in order to chart a fresh path forward into the goodness of God, in *Our Good Crisis: Overcoming Moral Chaos with the Beatitudes of Jesus* (IVP [US], 2020).

36 See the interview by Simon Mayo and Mark Kermode with Adam Curtis about his documentary *Can't Get You Out of My Head: An Emotional History of the Modern World*; https://www.youtube.com/watch?v=5eRrZifFkHA (accessed Feb. 17 2022).

37 Andrew Walls, *The Missionary Movement in Christian History* (Orbis Books, 1996), p 235.

38 John Stott, *Preaching Between Two Worlds* (Eerdmans, 2017).

39 See John Frame, *The Doctrine of the Knowledge of God* (P&R, 1987), as well as the rest of the volumes in his systematic theology series.

40 There is some debate regarding the claims and origin of the Colossian philosophy. It is probably a catchall term referring to influences ranging from a confident Jewish apologetic to syncretism with Hellenistic philosophy leading to some form of Gnosticism.

41 This is precisely what Robin DiAngelo, author of the well-known book *White Fragility*, proposes in her earlier co-authored book with Özlem Sensoy, *Is Everyone Really Equal?: An Introduction to Key Concepts in Social Justice Education*, Multicultural Education Series (Teachers College Press, 2017), Kindle Edition.

42 This refers to a scene in *The Matrix* (1999), where the protagonist is offered the choice between a red pill and a blue pill. If he takes the red pill, he will learn a potentially unsettling or life-changing truth. If he takes the blue pill, he can remain in contented ignorance.

43 Winn Collier, *A Burning in My Bones: An Authorized Biography of Eugene H. Peterson* (Crown Publishing, 2021), p 185, 283.

44 The present middle indicative verb conveys a certain action with personal agency.

45 Of course, God expresses his refreshment through us, but that happens most effectively when we embrace God as refreshing living water (John 7:37-39; Revelation 22:1-2) and as our nourishing pastor (Psalm 23:1-3; Ezekiel 34:13-16). A well-pastored pastor has much to give his flock.

46 To be sure, some people are gifted in evangelism (Ephesians 4:11). They have a particular knack and boldness in proclaiming the gospel to non-Christians. But too often evangelists operate as if their ministry is like a planet orbiting the church, drawing people to themselves or their message but not necessarily to church. But a gifted evangelist should view their ministry as more like a satellite launched from the church, traveling out into the unbelieving space, to return and draw people into the church. The gospel itself does not only save us for the Head but also into his Body. All leaders are called to do gospel work.

47 Robert Yarbrough, *The Letters to Timothy and Titus*, (Eerdmans, 2018), p 441.

48 There are countless ways to share the gospel. The Bible uses many metaphors to communicate the gospel. Jesus used agricultural metaphors to engage the attention of villagers, legal language for law experts, and water for the thirsty. Paul used theological terms that appealed to the deep needs of every human. Good evangelists will communicate the eternal, unchanging gospel into changing cultural forms. For more, see my book, *The Unbelievable Gospel: Say Something Worth Believing* (Zondervan, 2014), p 123-189.

49 William T. Cavanaugh, *Field Hospital: The Church's Engagement with a Wounded World* (Grand Rapids, MI: Eerdmans, 2016).